Easy Holiday CRAFTS™

Edited by Laura Scott

HOUSE of WHITE BIRCHES

PUBLISHERS SINCE 1947

Editor: Laura Scott
Pattern Editor: Läna Schurb
Associate Editor: June Sprunger
Copy Editor: Cathy Reef

Photography: Tammy Christian, Nora Elsesser
Photography Assistants: Linda Quinlan, Arlou Wittwer

Production Manager: Vicki Macy
Book Design/Production: Ronda Bollenbacher
Cover Design: Dan Kraner
Traffic Coordinator: Sandra Beres
Production Assistants: Dana Brotherton, Carol Dailey, Cheryl Lynch, Miriam Zacharias

Publishers: Carl H. Muselman, Arthur K. Muselman
Chief Executive Officer: John Robinson
Marketing Director: Scott Moss
Editorial Director: Vivian Rothe
Production Director: Scott Smith

Printed in the United States of America
First Printing: 1998
Library of Congress Number: 97-78423
ISBN: 1-882138-34-1

Every effort has been made to ensure the accuracy and completeness of the instructions in this book. However, we cannot be responsible for human error or for the results when using materials other than those specified in the instructions, or for variations in individual work.

The following models are from Charmaine Model Agency, Fort Wayne, Ind., Alexis Chaney, page 23, 79, 165; Kim Wohlfeil, page 135.

From the Editor

It used to be that for most people, Christmas was the only major gift-giving and decorating occasion of the year. In recent years however, as people everywhere have started to focus on the smaller holidays, crafting has had a more important part in our celebrations. Nowadays, it's not unusual to see co-workers giving one another hand-crafted Valentine's Day gifts, whimsical sprigs of green dressing up our St. Patrick's Day outfits, colorful Easter egg trees, patriotic accents, and cheery Halloween and Thanksgiving decorations indoors and out, in addition to oodles of Christmas accents and gifts galore!

The beauty of crafting is that you can celebrate the year's holidays with cards, gifts and decorations, all with minimal time and effort, depending on your crafting style and limitations. As you page through this book, you'll find that many, if not most of these projects can be made with crafting supplies you already have in your hobby room or craft closet.

From fabric and wood painting, sewing and no-sew projects, simple sculpting, paper crafting, floral arranging and much more, our hope is that you find this collection of crafts, from whimsical and heart-warming to elegant and enchanting, a delight to create and share with your friends and family throughout the year.

Warm regards,

Laura Scott

Laura Scott
Editor, *Easy Holiday Crafts*

Contents

Chapter 1: Bring in the New Year

Chapter 2: Valentine Treats for Sweethearts

Chapter 3: Luck o' the Irish

Chapter 4: Easter Fun & Surprises

Chapter 5: Just for Mom & Dad

Chapter 6: An American Celebration

Chapter 7: Tricks & Treats

Chapter 8: A Day of Thanks

Chapter 9: Happy Hanukkah

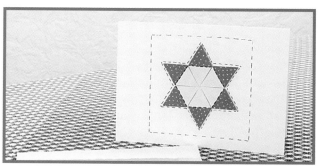

Chapter 10: A Merry Christmas

General Instructions

Materials Lists

In addition to the materials listed for each craft, some of the following crafting supplies may be needed to complete your projects. No doubt most of these are already on hand in your "treasure chest" of crafting aids. If not, you may want to gather them now so that you'll be able to complete each design quickly and without a hitch!

For General Crafts

- Scissors
- Pencil
- Ruler
- Tracing paper
- Craft knife
- Heavy-duty craft cutters or wire nippers

For Fabric Projects ▲

- Iron
- Ironing board
- Pressing cloth
- Basic sewing notions
- Rotary cutter and self-healing mat
- Air-soluble markers
- Tailor's chalk

For Needlework Designs

- Embroidery scissors
- Iron
- Ironing board
- Thick terry towel
- Air-soluble markers
- Tailor's chalk

◀ **For Painted Items**

- Paper towels
- Paper or plastic foam plate or tray to use as a disposable paint palette for holding and mixing paints
- Plastic—a garbage bag, grocery sack, etc.—to protect your work surface
- Container of water for rinsing and cleaning brushes

Reproducing Patterns & Templates

The patterns provided in this book are shown right side up, as they should look on the finished project; a few oversize patterns need to be enlarged are clearly marked. Photocopiers with enlarging capabilities are readily available at copy stores and office supply stores. Simply copy the page, setting the photocopy machine to enlarge the pattern to the percentage indicated.

Patterns which do not need to be enlarged can be reproduced simply by placing a piece of tracing paper or vellum over the pattern in the book, and tracing the outlines carefully with a pencil or other market.

Once you've copied your pattern pieces, cut them out and use these pieces as templates to trace around. Secure them as needed with pins or pattern weights.

If you plan to reuse the patterns or if the patterns are more intricate with sharp points, etc., make sturdier templates by gluing the copied page of patterns onto heavy cardboard or template plastic. Let the glue dry, then cut out the pieces using a craft knife.

Depending on the application, it may be preferable to trace the patterns onto the *wrong* side of the fabric or other material so that no tracing lines will be visible front the front; in this case, make sure you place the *right* side of the pattern piece against the *wrong* side of the fabric, paper or whatever so that the piece will face the right direction when it is cut out.

Working With Fabrics

Read instructions carefully; take seam allowanced into consideration when cutting fabrics.

If colorfastness is a concern, launder fabrics first without using fabric softener. Press with an iron before using. Keep an iron and ironing board at hand to press seams and pattern pieces as you work.

Pattern markings can be transferred to fabrics with air-soluble markers or tailor's chalk. For permanent markings on fabric, use the specific pens and paints listed with each project. It is a good idea to always test the pen or marker on a scrap of fabric to check for bleeding, etc.

Painted Designs

Disposable paper or plastic foam plates, including supermarket meat trays, make good palettes for pouring and mixing paints.

The success of a painted project often depends a great deal on the care taken in the initial preparations, including sanding, applying primer, and/or applying a base coat of color. Follow instructions carefully in this regard.

Take special care when painting adjacent sections different colors; allow the first color to dry so that the second will not run or mix. When adding designs atop a painted base, let the base coat dry thoroughly first.

If you will be mixing media, such as drawing with marking pens on a painted surface, test the process and your materials on scraps to make sure there will be no unsightly running or bleeding.

Keep your work surface and your tools clean. Clean brushes promptly in the manner recommended by the paint manufacturer; many acrylics can be cleaned up with soap and water, while other paints may require a solvent of some kind. Suspend your paintbrushes by their handles to dry so that the cleaning fluid drains out completely without bending the bristles. ▲

Bring in the New Year

As you count down the last seconds of this year, be sure to surround yourself with good friends and good wishes! This first chapter of Easy Holiday Crafts *brings you delightful New Year's gifts, a colorful party sign and whimsical party hats, horns and decorations!*

Shake, Rattle & Ring in the New Year!

Budget a little tight at December's end? No need to skimp on the party fun—save a bundle by making your own colorful party hats, noisemakers—even those paper blow-outs you loved as a kid! See photo on previous pages and at lower right.

Materials

Noisemaker

- Spiral wire from old notebook
- Assorted ribbons
- Jingle bells
- Washers

Party Hat

- Wrapping paper
- Paper grocery sacks or cereal boxes (optional)
- Pattern-edge paper scissors (optional)
- Foil and/or backs of foil-finish greeting cards or cardboard
- Assorted bows, ribbons, glitzy shreds, tinsel, garland, etc.
- Old greeting cards with holiday motifs
- Stapler
- Tape
- Craft glue

Party Blow-Out

- Cardboard tube from wrapping paper, paper towels or bathroom tissue
- Wrapping paper
- Colorful gift-wrapping tissue
- Beading wire
- Tape
- Craft glue

Noisemaker

Instructions

1. Trim all paper and cardboard covers from spiral wire.

2. Open one end of wire and slide on jingle bells and washers. Close wire end and attach it to other end to form a spiral circle.

3. Tie ribbon streamers onto the wire; tie jingle bells to the ends of some streamers.

Party Hat

Instructions

1. Glue together two large sheets of wrapping paper—identical or different—with their wrong sides facing. Recycle paper grocery sacks or cereal boxes for the lining, if you prefer.

2. Fold paper into cone to fit head; staple, glue and tape edge neatly so hat will maintain its shape. Trim edge neatly using pattern-edge paper scissors—scallops, zigzags, etc., as desired.

3. Decorate hat with your choice of cut-out motifs from holiday cards, designs cut from foil or foil-finish paper or cardboard (see templates on page 11), bows, ribbons, glitter, etc.

4. To add streamers, roll an 8" strip of tape upon itself, sticky side out. Press on sparkly streamers or shreds. Stick tape down inside tip of hat so streamers flow out the top.

Party Blow-Out

Instructions

1. Make a straight cut the length of the cardboard tube. Cut tube across its width into 5" sections. Roll sections back on themselves to make tubes 1" in diameter. Tape or glue to secure.

2. For each blow-out, cut a piece of tissue paper 3½" x 20". Lay tissue facedown. For curling support, tape a 20" length of beading wire down the center of the tissue on the wrong side. Fold tissue lengthwise into thirds, folding both sides toward center and over wire.

3. Glue tissue paper along its length, leaving an open tissue-paper tube, to within about 3" of one end. Insert the cardboard tube in this end. Fit tissue snugly around tube and complete gluing. Fold over other end about ½" and glue or tape to close tightly.

**New Year's Hats
Templates**

Fold

Fold

4. Wrap cardboard tube with wrapping paper. Decorate with assorted ribbons, stickers, seals, glitter, etc. Let blower dry completely.

5. Once glue is completely dry, carefully roll tissue toward tube. To use, blow into open end of cardboard tube. ■

—*Designs by Louy Danube*

New Year's Celebration

Here's a colorful decoration to welcome in the new year. You'll find it fun to punch and easy to paint in bright, bold colors.

Materials

- 9" x 11" sheet aluminum flashing*
- Tin snips
- Several finishing nails
- Large nail
- Hammer
- Enamel paints: white, black, red, yellow, green, blue and brown
- Gold-glitter fabric paint
- Small paintbrush
- Fine-line black permanent marker
- Pen
- Masking tape
- Tacky craft glue
- 14" multicolored wire garland
- 10 (6mm) diamond-color rhinestones

Aluminum flashing is widely available at hardware stores.

Instructions

1. Work on a hard, protective surface, such as a pressed-wood board. Place tracing paper over pattern (page 13). Trace with pen; cut out paper pattern.

2. Place paper pattern on aluminum; trace with pen. Cut out shape with tin snips. Place aluminum on work surface. Tape paper pattern in place over aluminum.

3. Punch design with hammer and finishing nail, moving from dot to dot and switching to a new nail when point becomes dull. Use larger nail to punch the two larger holes on top and right stars as indicated.

4. Remove paper and tape; turn aluminum over. (Smooth side is the back.)

5. Mix white and black paints to make gray; mix white and red to make pink; and mix white with brown to achieve a cork tan.

6. Referring to pattern and photo, paint design with thick strokes, painting just inside the punched lines. Let dry.

7. Squeeze or brush gold-glitter paint over yellow stars. Allow all paints to dry thoroughly.

8. Using permanent black fine-line marker and referring to Lettering Diagram, add "Happy New Year." Referring to photo, glue five rhinestones over each eye. Thread garland through larger holes; twist ends. ■

—*Design by Sandra Graham Smith*

New Year's Celebration

Lettering Diagram

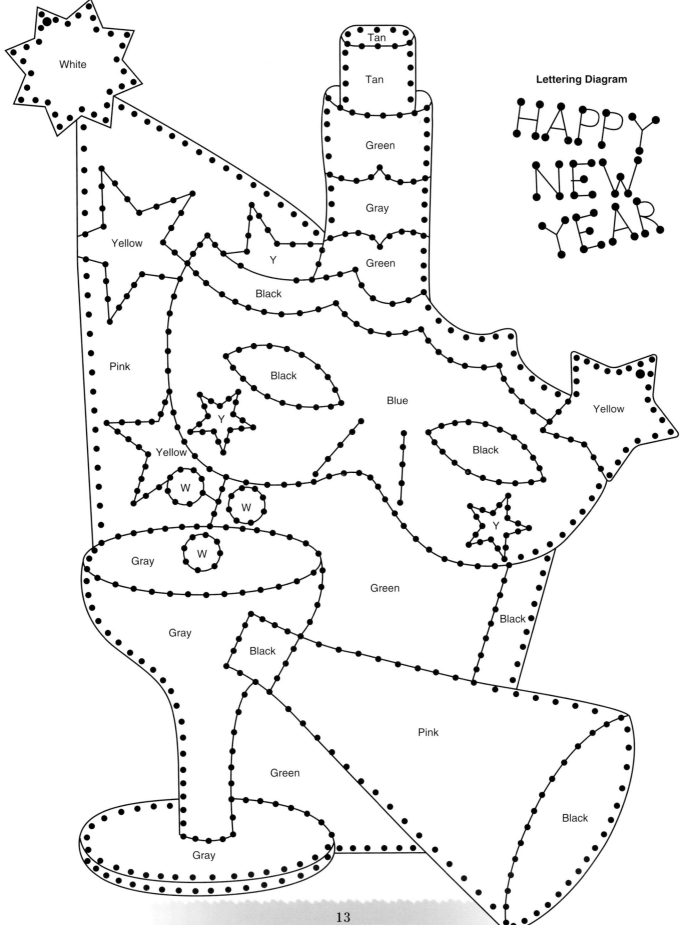

Happy Moo Year

Cows are so popular—you're sure to know several people who love to collect and decorate with bovine buddies! Here's a great addition to their collection.

Materials

- 14-count plastic canvas
- Anchor 6-strand embroidery floss as listed in color key
- Kreinik ⅟16" Ribbon as listed in color key
- Stuffed cow from A Bear in Sheep's Clothing
- Craft glue
- Dress It Up Vineyard button-and-charm packet from Jesse James & Co.
- Coordinating green felt or synthetic suede

Instructions

1. Cut plastic canvas according to graph. Using 6 strands embroidery floss, stitch as shown.

2. Using gold metallic ⅟16" ribbon, Overcast edges, holding ribbon at an angle to keep it flat and smooth and stitching through corner holes two or three times as needed to cover plastic canvas.

3. Stitch two loops of twisted cord to back at right and left sides of sign.

4. Applying glue sparingly, glue felt or synthetic suede to back of stitched piece. Referring to photo, glue miniature champagne bottle, grapes buttons, grapes charm, leaves and buttons to front of sign.

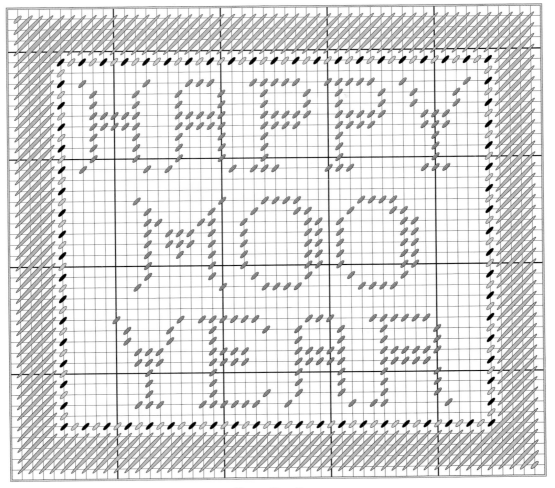

Happy Moo Year
50 holes x 44 holes
Cut 1

5. Slip loops of sign over cow's front legs. Glue purple ribbon bow around cow's neck; embellish bow with leaf and purple button from embellishments packet. ■

—Design by Judi Kauffman

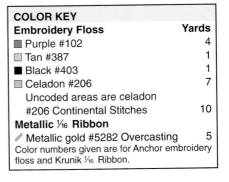

COLOR KEY

Embroidery Floss	Yards
■ Purple #102	4
☐ Tan #387	1
■ Black #403	1
☐ Celadon #206	7
Uncoded areas are celadon #206 Continental Stitches	10
Metallic ⅟₁₆ Ribbon	
⁄ Metallic gold #5282 Overcasting	5

Color numbers given are for Anchor embroidery floss and Krunik ⅟₁₆ Ribbon.

Valentine Treats for Sweethearts

Fill the 14th of February with romance and love! The perfect way to express your love is through a handcrafted gift. Whether it's a candy-filled basket, a conversation hearts wreath, homemade cards, a sweet pin or another tenderly crafted item, your loved ones are sure to feel extra-special!

Sweetheart Wreath

In bright candy colors, those old-fashioned "conversation hearts" get a make-over in this fun craft project. Paint wooden hearts in cool colors and add messages that are completely up to date! See photo on previous pages.

Materials

- 21" x 4" piece of ¾"-thick wood
- Ceramcoat acrylic paints from Delta Technical Coatings—pretty pink, crocus yellow, phthalo blue, Bahama purple, pink quartz, nectar coral, bright red and sweetheart blush
- Paintbrushes
- Paint palette or paper plate
- Scroll saw or band saw
- Sandpaper
- Drill
- Graphite paper
- Clear acrylic sealer with glossy finish
- Sponge
- 1½ yards fence wire
- Wire cutters
- Fat pencil or ½" dowel
- 3 small buttons
- 6" ¾"-wide white lace
- Natural-color raffia
- Hot-glue gun
- Liquid glue stick
- Fine white glitter
- Hard-lead pencil
- Black felt-tip pen

Instructions

1. Trace patterns; cut out. Place graphite paper graphite side down on wood; place patterns right side up on top of graphite paper. Using hard-lead pencil, transfer heart outlines. Cut out with scroll saw or band saw; sand edges smooth.

2. Paint one heart crocus yellow, one phthalo blue, one pink quartz, and one nectar coral. Let hearts dry overnight.

3. Place graphite paper on painted hearts. Using pencil, lightly transfer lettering onto wood. Using pretty pink, paint lettering on all hearts; let dry.

4. On yellow and blue hearts, paint over the lettering with sweetheart blush. On pink and coral hearts, paint over lettering with bright red. Let dry. Using black felt-tip pen, outline letters with dash-dot pattern; add fine wavy dash-dot border as in photo.

5. Dip sponge in Bahama purple; pat off excess paint onto paper. Referring to photo, lightly sponge paint onto blue and coral hearts. Using bright red, repeat sponging process on yellow and pink hearts. Set aside to dry overnight.

6. Drill holes in hearts where indicated. Referring to photo, thread 3-foot piece of wire into hole on blue heart; curl end into a loop to hold wire in place. (Loop should protrude from front.) Bring wire behind heart to bottom of heart and slightly to the right; loosely wrap it four or five times around pencil or dowel. Thread wire from front to back through right-hand hole of coral heart, across back, and then back through left-hand hole. Loosely wrap wire three or four times around pencil. Run wire through right-hand hole, then left-hand hole in yellow heart. Loosely wrap wire around pencil once or twice before passing it up the back of the pink heart. Thread from back through hole to front. Snip off, curling wire into a loop to hold it in place.

7. Loosely wrap 18" piece of wire around pencil, leaving ¾" straight ends. Bend one end around wreath wire behind pink heart and the other end around wire behind blue heart.

8. Tie raffia into a bow; tie to top center of wire wreath. Referring to photo, glue buttons to upper right and upper left hearts.

9. Trace "Love Ya" on coral heart with liquid glue; sprinkle liberally with fine glitter. Shake off excess. Apply glue all over pink heart *except* the "Love Bug" lettering; apply glitter and shake off excess.

10. Tie two bows from lace; referring to photo, glue to yellow and blue hearts. ♥

—Design by Chris Brack

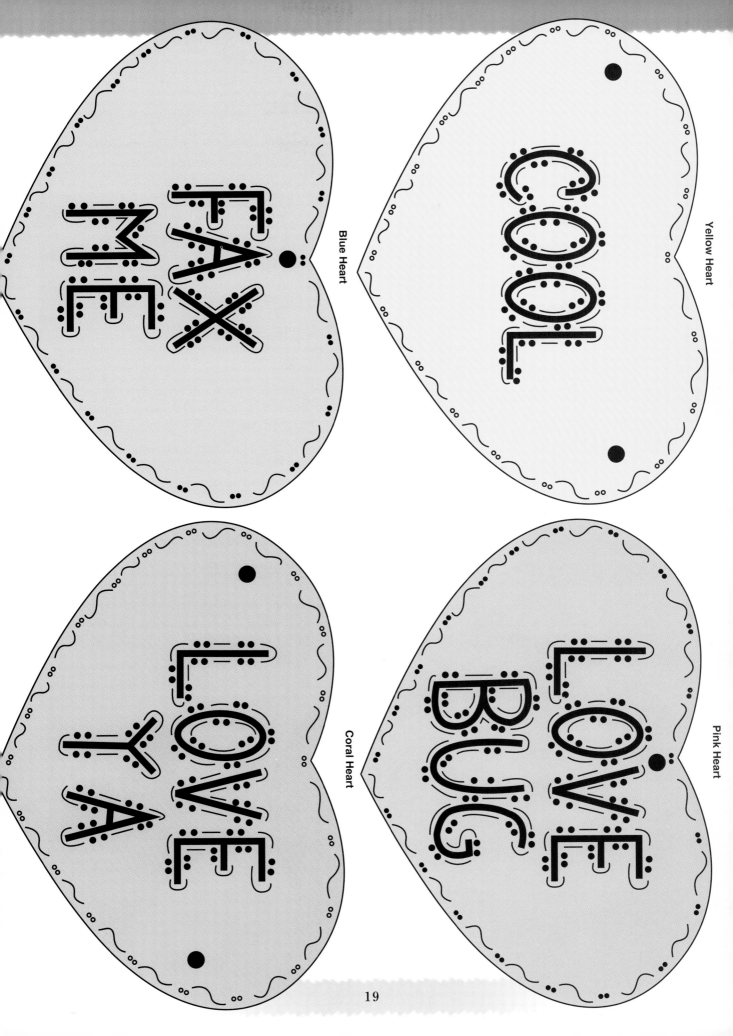

Blue Heart

FAX ME

Yellow Heart

COOL

Coral Heart

LOVE YA

Pink Heart

LOVE BUG

19

Love Frame

If you love the look of silk ribbon embroidery but haven't the time or inclination to learn all those stitches, here's the project for you! Ready-made appliqués of embroidered silk ribbon make a lovely, old-fashioned decorating accent.

Materials

- Simply Stitches silk-ribbon–embroidery appliqués from Westwater Enterprises
- Frame with curved glass
- Cardboard (sample is 10" x 9")
- Polyester batting
- Fabric for background (sample is 10" x 9")
- Programmable sewing machine
- Variegated pink rayon sewing thread
- Air-soluble marking pen
- Low-temperature glue gun
- Fabric glue
- Craft cement

Project Notes

Any frame with a curved glass will do. For a smaller frame, choose smaller ribbon appliqués and narrower trim. For larger openings, choose larger appliqués or a combination of several smaller ones and larger trim.

If you do not have access to a programmable sewing machine, you may embroider the message with needle and embroidery floss.

Instructions

1. Remove frame backing; place on lightweight paper. Trace; cut out.

2. Place paper pattern on cardboard. Trace again; cut out cardboard. Slip cardboard into opening to check fit, trimming as necessary.

3. Place cardboard on fabric; trace with air-soluble pen. Referring to photo throughout, plan placement of appliqués and stitched message within outline. Using programmed sewing machine or stitching by hand, stitch "Love" or other message.

4. Cut out fabric ½" larger than traced shape all around.

5. Place cardboard on batting; trace and cut two shapes from batting.

6. Stack batting pieces atop cardboard. Center fabric over batting, wrong side facing batting. Smoothly wrap fabric edges around to back; glue with glue gun.

7. Using fabric glue, glue silk ribbon appliqués in place. Insert panel in frame opening; secure in place with craft cement.

—Design by Beth Wheeler

Cupid Magnet

Give someone you love this sweet little treasure as a constant reminder that you hold them close in your heart! It's fun to mold the pieces from modeling compound—you can turn out several in a very short time!

Materials

- Sculpey III modeling compound:
  Red #082
  Flesh #092
  Ivory #501
- 2 black seed beads
- Acrylic mini-curl hair in color of your choice
- Scrap of ⅛"-wide burgundy ribbon
- ½" round magnet
- Straight-edge tool for cutting and making lines
- Hot-glue gun
- Craft glue
- Clean white rag
- Black permanent marker (optional)

Instructions

1. Cut off ⅛ of the red modeling compound. Roll it into a ball between the palms of your hands.

2. Flatten ball into teardrop shape with a pointed end and one round end. Pat and work compound to flatten teardrop to uniform ¼" thickness. With straight edge, make a cut in rounded end for top of heart. Continue working with compound until you have achieved desired heart shape.

3. Clean hands thoroughly on a white rag to remove any traces of color before working with other colors.

4. Cut off ¹⁄₁₆ of the flesh modeling compound for head. Soften and roll it into a ball, then pat it into a uniform ¼"-thick circle.

5. Referring to photo, press black seed beads on their sides into head for eyes; press until none of the bead hole shows. Using straight edge, indent two eyelashes for each eye (Fig. 1).

Fig. 1

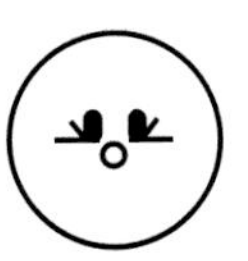

6. Rub your finger into a little of the red modeling compound and transfer the coloring from your fingertip to each cheek for blush.

7. Center head atop heart. Roll a tiny, tiny ball of flesh modeling compound and press gently in place for nose.

8. Form two pea-size balls of flesh-color compound. Roll each into a rope about 1⅛" long with one end thicker than the other; compare them to insure that the thick ends are the same width.

9. Flatten and round the thick end of each for hands. Attach one hand to one side of heart, attaching arm on back of heart below head; trim off any excess. Repeat with other arm. Arms should touch bottom of head on back and should meet in center on back.

10. Soften, roll and flatten two pea-size balls of ivory compound into teardrop shapes for wings. With straight edge, press three lines into each (Fig. 2). Attach wings by pressing them onto backs of arms.

Fig. 2

11. Transfer molded magnet to an oven-proof plate. Bake in a preheated 275-degree oven for 10 minutes; cool completely.

12. Cut three or four ½" strands of hair; rub between fingers to get them to stick together. Glue hair to top of head. Cut two ¼" strands of hair and glue them to head toward back center so that they stand up.

13. Make a tiny bow from burgundy ribbon and glue onto hair, in front of the two strands that are standing up.

14. Glue magnet to back in center directly below arms. Add a message to heart with permanent black marker, if desired. ❤

—Design by Jackie Haskell

Mommy's Little Sweetheart

Cuddly as a hug from Mama—that's this darling little zip-up jacket made in a wink from pretty fabric remnants and a ready-made sweatshirt!

Materials
- White child's size sweatshirt (see Project Note)
- 14" white jacket zipper (see Project Note)
- Fabric:
  - ¼ yard green stripe
  - ¼ yard pink-and-green floral
  - ¼ yard pink-and-green plaid
- Rotary cutter
- Self-healing mat
- Coordinating sewing threads
- ⅜"-wide elastic

Project Notes

Choose a sweatshirt at least one size larger than you would normally buy. Sample project uses a size 10–12 sweatshirt for a finished size 8–10 jacket.

Sample jacket uses a 14" zipper; larger or shorter jacket may require zipper of a different size.

Stitch with a ¼" seam allowance unless otherwise noted.

Instructions

1. Measure child's sleeve length from neck to wrist; cut sleeves this length. Measure child's front from neck to waist; cut hem this length. Cut sweatshirt open along center front line.

2. Fold top point of neck ribbing down to sweatshirt (see Fig. 1). Stitch in place with narrow zigzag stitch.

Fig. 1
Fold
Zigzag

3. Cut 1½"-wide strip across fabric width from plaid fabric. Cut two 2½"-wide strips across fabric width from both green stripe and pink floral.

4. Stitch one striped strip to one floral strip along long edge, right sides facing. Repeat with remaining 2½"-wide strips. Press seam allowances toward floral fabric.

5. Cut units sewn together in Step 4 in 2½" slices. Stitch slices together to form two checkerboard bands long enough to fit around hem edge. Stitch bands together with alternating squares; press seam allowances in one direction.

6. Stitch remaining slices together in two pairs for elbow patches.

7. Stitch plaid strip along one long edge of checkerboard hem band. Turn raw edge of plaid strip under ½". Place checkerboard hem band right side up along hem edge of sweatshirt with raw edges even. Pin along raw edges and along fold of plaid border; stitch along hem with blind-hem or zigzag stitch. Press.

8. Turn edges of each elbow patch under ⅜"–½"; press. Position on sleeves; pin. Stitch in place with blind-hem or zigzag stitch. Press.

9. Cut a 2"-wide strip of plaid fabric to fit around jacket hem edge. Press under ½" along one long edge. Stitch other long edge along hem of jacket with right sides facing. Fold to wrong side, creating a casing. Stitch along fold with zigzag stitch. Insert elastic to fit comfortably around child's waist. Stitch across each end of casing, securing ends of elastic.

10. Repeat step 9 for sleeves with elastic to fit comfortably around child's wrist, plus ½" for overlap.

11. Cut two 1½"-wide strips of plaid fabric across fabric width. Cut each strip in half to make four strips, each 1½" by half of fabric width.

12. Place two strips together, right sides facing with zipper tape between, long edges even and zipper tape top easing out (Fig. 2). Stitch along raw edge and across each end. Trim corners; turn right side out (Fig. 3, page 27). Press.

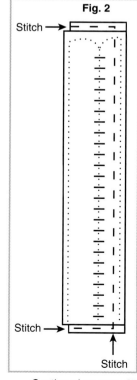

Fig. 2

Stitch →

Stitch →

Stitch

Continued on page 27

Mommy's Little Sweetheart

Woven Heartstrings Vest

Instructions begin on page 24

Woven Heartstrings Vest

If the last thing you wove was one of those stretchy-loop pot holders, it's time to give it another try! Just weave colorful calico strips like a lattice pie crust and cut them into shapes that you accent with fabric paints! See photo on page 23.

Materials

- BagWorks blue denim vest with lapels
- ¼ yard each of 2 coordinating calico fabrics in colors desired for hearts
- Scraps of green print calico
- Fusible transfer webbing
- Duncan Scribbles dimensional fabric paints: green and copper (or colors to coordinate with your fabric choices)
- Straight pins
- Rotary cutter with wave blade

Project Notes

Woven strips should fit tightly against each other to completely cover the fusible webbing.

A vest size extra-large was used for the sample project.

Instructions

1. Cut fusible webbing 11½" x 17½"; place adhesive side up on ironing board.

2. Using rotary cutter fitted with wave blade, cut 10 (½"-wide) strips across fabric width from each of the two coordinating calicos.

3. Cut strips of one of the calicoes in half. Referring to Fig. 1, lay strips across fusible webbing, pinning ends in place.

4. Cut each strip of other calico into thirds. Weave first strip over and under strips already pinned to fusible webbing; weave second strip under and over, and so on, until all strips are used and fusible webbing is completely covered.

5. Remove pins. Following manufacturer's instructions, fuse webbing to woven fabric. Trim edges of fabric even with webbing.

6. Referring to patterns, cut eight large hearts and six small hearts from fused woven fabric.

Continued on page 29

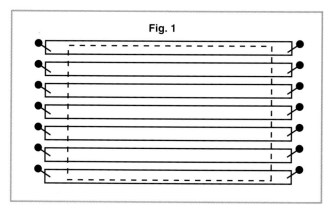

Fig. 1

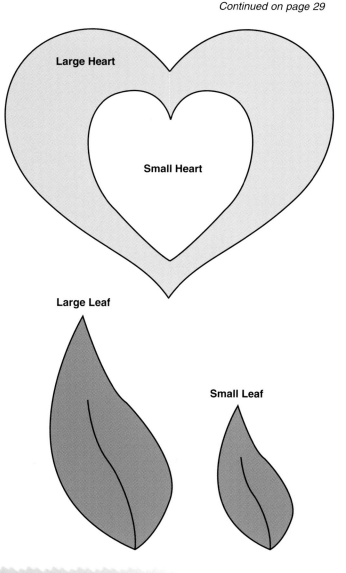

Large Heart

Small Heart

Large Leaf

Small Leaf

You're All Heart

Raid your stash of fabric for bright scraps, add a dab of dimensional craft paint, and you have the makings for a charming card that works equally well as a special valentine, a thank-you card or an all-purpose note.

Materials

- 5" x 7" blank card stock
- Fusible webbing
- Fabric scraps in 4 bright colors/patterns
- Gold dimensional craft paint
- Red calligraphy pen or marking pen

Instructions

1. Following manufacturer's instructions, fuse webbing to wrong sides of fabrics. Referring to photo, cut four hearts in graduating sizes from fabrics.

2. Position hearts on front of card; fuse hearts to card front; let cool.

3. Write "You're All Heart" or other message on front of card with red pen.

4. Outline hearts with gold dimensional craft paint. Set aside to dry completely. ♥

—Design by Blanche Lind

Fast & Easy Sachets

Assembly-line efficiency is the key to making dozens of these cuties in a hurry! Vary the fabric and shape to make lovely designs for all seasons. Fill them with potpourri, cotton balls scented with your favorite cologne, scented guest soaps or aromatic bath beads.

Materials
Makes 5

- 45" lace
- 5" piece of 44"- or 45"-wide muslin
- Hot-glue gun
- Fusible webbing
- Fabric scraps
- Assorted bows
- Assorted buttons
- 5 (13") pieces coordinating ribbon
- Assorted pony beads or other beads
- Sewing machine with zigzag option
- White sewing thread

Instructions

1. Zigzag lace to top edge of muslin.

2. On wrong side of fabric, mark off consecutive 4" sections. Cut apart at every other line. Fold each piece in half, wrong sides facing; press. Open and lay right side up.

3. Iron fusible webbing onto backs of fabric scraps. Referring to template, trace heart sections onto fabrics. Cut out pieces. Match heart sections and iron to fronts of sachets.

4. Refold sachets, right sides facing. Stitch bottom and side using ¼" seam allowance. Turn bag right side out. Glue on buttons and bows as desired.

5. Thread beads onto both ends of 13" ribbon; knot to hold beads in place. Use ribbon to tie top of sachet closed. ❤

—*Design by Louy Danube*

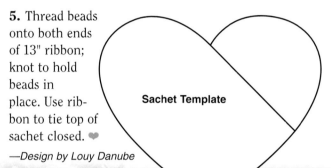

Sachet Template

Valentine Wreath

Add a touch of springtime color to even the smallest space with this diminutive wreath. By observing a few simple design principles, you can create your own floral masterpieces of silk or dried flowers in any color combination that pleases you.

Materials
- Small straw or grapevine heart-shaped wreath
- Deep pink silk rosebuds
- Smaller bright pink silk blossoms for accents
- Silk white baby's breath for filler
- Silk ivy for background
- Low-temperature glue gun
- Thin floral wire

Project Notes

Though this wreath is small, it uses basic floral design principles and techniques. You can apply them to almost any floral composition.

Start with a greenery background; add featured blossoms in groups of three, five or seven. Accent with smaller blossoms and finish with filler material for a full arrangement.

If arrangement will hang or be viewed straight on, the top of the wreath will be most important. If arrangement will sit in the center of a table or other flat surface at eye level, wreath sides will be equally important.

The sample project shown here uses a straw base covered on the sides and front with silk leaves.

Instructions

1. Glue short pieces of ivy all around grapevine wreath.

2. Glue rosebuds and leaves spaced evenly around wreath.

3. Tuck accent blossoms around each rosebud cluster, under foliage.

4. Remove small clusters of filler flowers from stems; glue under and around each cluster of blossoms to achieve desired fullness.

5. Weave wire hanging loop into back of wreath. ♥

—Design by Beth Wheeler

Mommy's Little Sweetheart

Continued from page 22

13. Place remaining two plaid strips together, right sides facing and remaining long edge of zipper tape between. Stitch along long edge and across each end. Trim corners; turn right side out. Press.

14. Place zipper facedown along left side of sweatshirt with raw edge of zipper facing even with raw edge of jacket front. Pin front layer of facing only to sweatshirt. Stitch with ½" seam allowance.

15. Fold facing to inside of sweatshirt, encasing raw edge at top and bottom of jacket. Turn raw edge under ½". Pin in place. Stitch along fold with narrow zigzag stitch.

16. Open zipper; apply zipper to right side of sweatshirt in similar manner. Press. ♥

—Design by Beth Wheeler

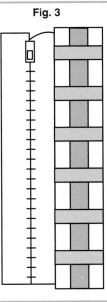

Fig. 3

Cupid & Heart Pin

Today's craft products make it easy to create brand-new jewelry with all the charm of much-loved antiques! That's the idea behind this novel brooch— fine for tucking into a valentine before you send it to someone special.

Materials

- Aleene's Enhancers paints and finishes:
  All-Purpose Primer #EN 104
  Matte Varnish #EN 107
- Aleene's Essentials:
  Ivory #OC 179
- Aleene's Premium-Coat Acrylics paints:
  Deep mauve #OC 104
  Dusty green #OC 141
- Creative Beginnings charms: picture frame and cupid
- Sandpaper
- Drill
- ¼" soft flat brush
- Small stiff-bristle brush
- Heavy decorative paper or small photo
- Hot-glue gun
- Needle-nose pliers
- Pin back
- Rusted tin from Bits & Pieces by Joan

Project Note

For best results, read all instructions before beginning. Refer to photo throughout for color placement.

Instructions

1. Sand charms lightly so paint will adhere.

2. Using heart template, cut heart shape from rusted tin with scissors. Sand edges smooth. Drill small hole at top center.

3. Using flat brush through step 4, apply primer to charms; let dry.

4. Paint frame ivory; let dry.

5. Dry-brush heart with deep mauve: Dip tip of stiff-bristle brush into undiluted paint. Wipe off almost all the paint

Heart Template

onto a paper towel. Brush over the surface with little or no pressure to create a softly textured, aged look. Repeat for more opaque coverage. Do not use water on the brush until you have finished layering the paint.

6. Using same method, dry-brush cupid and edges of heart with ivory, and frame with dusty green. Let dry.

7. Using flat brush, apply matte varnish to each piece.

8. Cut decorative paper or favorite photo to fit in frame. Place frame backing on back of paper or photo; press in sides of back of frame to hold it firmly in place. Glue pin back to back of frame; let dry.

9. Using needle-nose pliers, attach heart and cupid to frame charm. ❤

—Design by Jennifer Blevins for Duncan Enterprises

Gold Doily Valentines

Few gifts are more special than handmade greeting cards! With odds and ends and just a few simple supplies, you can craft spectacular creations to rival the fanciest—and most outrageously expensive—store-bought valentines!

Materials

- 12" x 5¼" ivory card stock
- 6" gold heart-shaped paper doily
- Craft glue
- Craft knife
- Pattern-edge paper scissors
- Reproduction decorative papers, old greeting cards, magazines or wrapping paper
- 8" wire-edge ribbon in color of your choice

Instructions

1. Using gold heart doily as a guide, pencil a heart outline on folded card stock, aligning top of heart with fold.

2. Using paper scissors with decorative edge, cut heart from card, cutting it slightly smaller than gold doily while maintaining two uncut areas along fold.

3. Trim out center of heart doily or leave in place, as you prefer. Glue doily to front of card.

4. Decorate doily with cutouts from decorative papers, magazines, greeting cards, magazines, etc. Tie ribbon in bow and glue to card. Add handwritten message to inside of card. ♥

—*Design by Louy Danube*

Woven Heartstrings

Continued from page 24

7. Bond webbing to wrong side of green calico. Cut three small leaves and six large leaves from fabric.

8. Remove paper backing from hearts and leaves. Referring to photo (page 23), arrange hearts and leaves on vest front. Fuse.

9. Outline hearts with copper dimensional paint; outline leaves with green. Let dry for at least one hour.

10. With green paint, add vines and center veins to leaves, and outline a few additional leaves in paint only. Let dry completely. ♥

—*Design by Beth Wheeler*

The Way to a Man's Heart

Win rave reviews for more than just the food when you serve your romantic Valentine's Day dinner in this special apron!

Materials

- White bib apron with pocket
- 15" piece 5"-wide gathered lace
- 1 yard white passementerie braid
- Kreinik Fine (#8) Braid: Star Pink #092
- Aleene's OK To Wash It Glue
- Seam sealant
- Assorted pink buttons
- Assorted silk ribbon rosettes, tiny ribbon bows, lace medallions and brass charms
- Sewing needle
- White sewing thread

Options

Start with a bright red apron and use pink lace, red and gold charms and buttons. Start with a natural apron and use crochet lace, country buttons and charms. Or make your own apron from a print fabric.

Instructions

1. Wash apron to remove sizing; press.

2. Sew or glue lace over pocket 1" from top of pocket, turning raw edges under ½" at sides. Using white thread and tiny stitches, sew ends in place.

3. Referring to photo throughout, arrange buttons and bows in random order across top of pocket, over gathered strip on lace. When you have a pleasing arrangement, sew buttons, rosettes and bows in place with a double strand of fine (#8) braid.

4. Using white thread, sew lace motifs and charms in place.

5. Referring to photo, sew or glue passementerie braid along sides of apron, leaving 1" at ends to turn to backside of apron. Apply seam sealant to cut ends of braid. ❤

—Design by Judi Kauffman

Beaded Heart Pin

Lustrous beads give this pretty pin the glow of a Victorian-style treasure.

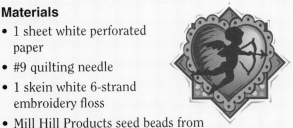

Materials

- 1 sheet white perforated paper
- #9 quilting needle
- 1 skein white 6-strand embroidery floss
- Mill Hill Products seed beads from Gay Bowles Sales Inc. as listed in color key
- 4" square Pellon fusible interfacing
- Pin back

Project Note

Beading is worked from left to right and the top down.

To begin, thread needle and knot end of thread. Pass needle through perforated paper from front to back 1" to the right of where you will attach the first bead. Referring to Beading Diagram, attach beads as shown on graph, taking care to work over the thread tail on back. When you reach the knot, carefully clip it off.

When you reach the end of a row, do not carry thread across the back to the beginning of the next row. Instead, either weave the thread tail back and forth under the stitches on the back and clip it, or run it back under the stitches you have just made to the beginning of the next row without clipping.

Maintain an even tension that holds the beads snug against the backing without puckering or cutting into the paper. Loose beads can be secured by run-ning the needle and thread under their stitches on the back.

Instructions

1. Cut a 4" square of perforated paper. Identify paper's right side; it is the smoother side. Find center of square; mark lightly on *wrong* side with pencil. Count up and to the left to find end of top row where first bead will be attached; mark on wrong side.

2. Cut 18" length of embroidery floss; separate into individual strands. Thread 1 strand onto needle.

3. Working as described in Project Notes, attach beads as shown on graph.

4. When all beads are attached, iron fusible interfacing onto back of design: Lay thick terry towel on ironing board. Place beaded piece right side down on towel; lay dot side of interfacing atop wrong side of beading. Iron in place.

5. With small scissors, trim away excess paper and interfacing in a decorative pattern of your choice, leaving a margin of at least one row of unworked paper around design.

6. Sew pin back onto back of design, taking care not to tear paper. ❤

—*Design by Rhonda Semonis*

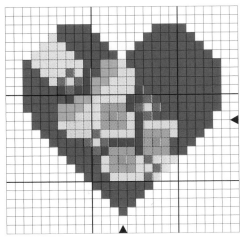

Beaded Heart Pin
23 beads x 22 beads

COLOR KEY	
Beads	**Packets**
☐ Yellow #128	1
☐ Light pink #145	1
☐ Light gray #150	1
■ Dark green #332	1
☐ White #479	1
■ Red #968	1
☐ Pink #2005	1
☐ Light blue #2007	
☐ Claret #2012	
Color numbers given are for Mill Hill seed beads.	

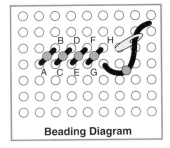

Beading Diagram

Luck o' the Irish

You'll feel as lucky as a leprechaun
when you begin to create the
delightful St. Patrick's Day
projects included in this chapter!
Whether you go all out for St.
Paddy's Day or simply wear
a sprig of green, you'll find 10
whimsical and wonderful projects
to help you celebrate!

Lucky Leprechaun

Check your stash or visit your favorite fabric store to find a fun shamrock print for this little fellow. Simple to make, he's light enough to hang on a door. He'll bring a smile to everyone he sees, Irish or otherwise! See photo on previous pages.

Materials

- Felt: kelly green, cinnamon and cream
- 12" square shamrock print fabric
- Stocking from pantyhose
- Polyester fiberfill
- Slick dimensional fabric paint: white, kelly green and red
- Sewing needle
- Coordinating sewing threads
- 4 yards Bumpy autumn hair from Fiber Mosaics
- Hot-glue gun
- 3" x 9½" green craft foam
- Black extra-fine-point permanent marking pen
- Powder blusher
- 2 metallic green shamrocks cut from a shamrock garland
- 1½" x 5½" piece cardboard
- Sewing machine

Instructions

1. Cut 6" x 5" piece from stocking. Round edges and gather by hand. Pull gathers and stuff head with stuffing; stitch closed.

2. Cut ¾"-diameter circle from stocking; gather and stuff. Sew closed and sew to face front for nose. Apply blusher to cheeks.

3. Referring to photo and using white dimensional paint, paint whites of leprechaun's eyes. Let dry. Paint green irises on eyes and red smile; let dry.

4. Following patterns (also see page 36) and adding ¼" seam allowance, cut two shirts from shamrock-print fabric and two pants from kelly green felt. With right sides together, sew shirt pieces together across top from cuff to cuff, and under each arm from cuff to waist. Sew pant leg seams from waist to cuff and inseams from cuff to cuff.

5. Turn shirt and pants right side out; stuff lightly.

6. Cut two shoes on the fold from cinnamon felt. Sew together with an Overcasting stitch from ankle to toe and ankle to heel. Stuff lightly.

7. Tuck pant legs neatly down inside shoes; sew in place with coordinating sewing thread.

8. Cut two hands from cream felt. Fold raw edges of shamrock fabric to inside around cuffs. Tuck felt hands into cuffs and stitch to secure.

9. Tuck raw shirt edge into pants at waist; glue or stitch.

10. Glue cardboard strip up back of leprechaun so it is not visible from front, making sure to attach cardboard to pants, shirt and head.

Happy St. Patrick's Day

Lucky Leprechaun Sign
Cut 1 from green craft foam

Lucky Leprechaun Hatbrim
Cut 1 from cinnamon felt

11. Cut strands of hair 3"–4" long for beard. Fold in half and glue to front of face. Cut strands of hair 6" long; tie in center. Glue to top of head at center front.

12. From cinnamon felt, cut hat brim and 3" x 8" strip for crown. Glue hatbrim circle to head. Overlap ends of crown to make circle; glue or stitch. Glue bottom edge of crown to hatbrim in an oval shape. Fold top edges of crown into corners; glue front center to back center to close top of hat.

13. Following pattern, cut sign from green craft foam. Write lettering with fine-point marker. Paint shamrocks on foam using green dimensional paint. Let dry. Glue ends of banner to hands.

14. From shamrock-print fabric, cut ½" x 8" strip for hatband. Glue around crown of hat, overlapping ends in back. Glue metallic shamrocks to left front of hat crown over hatband. Cut small squares from print fabric; glue to knees of pants. ❖

—*Design by Janna Britton*

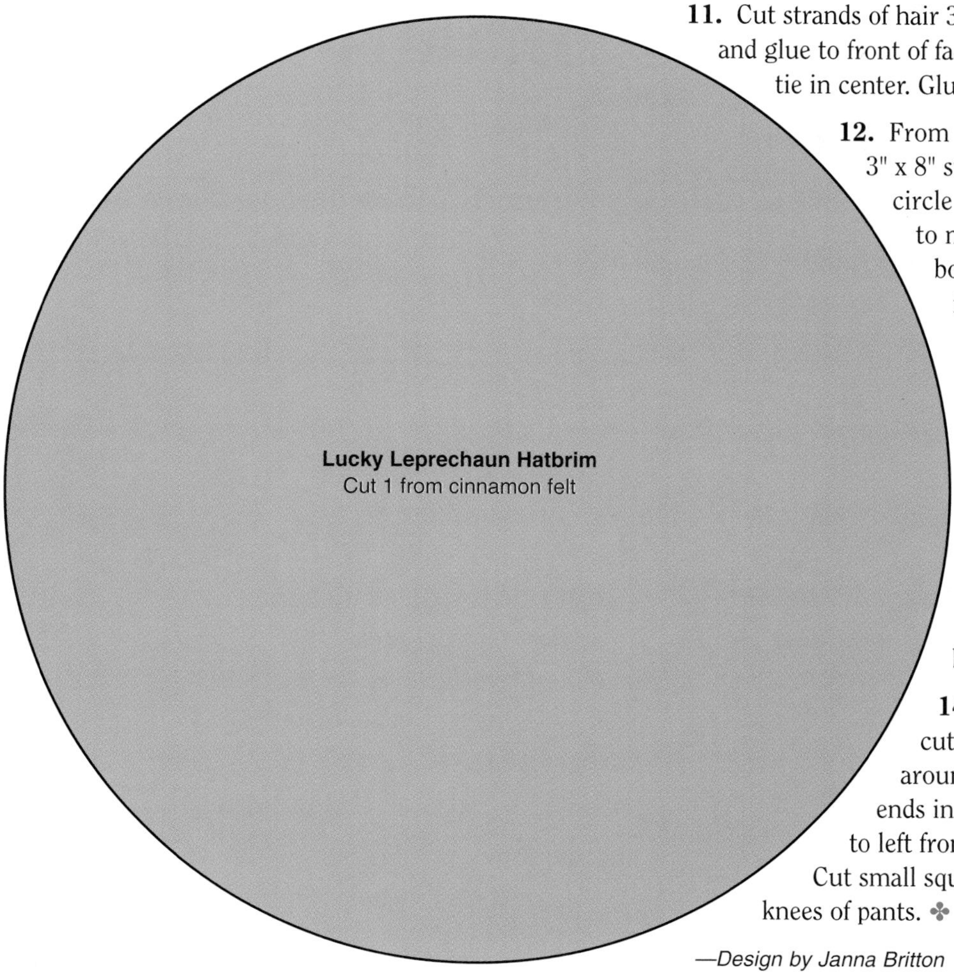

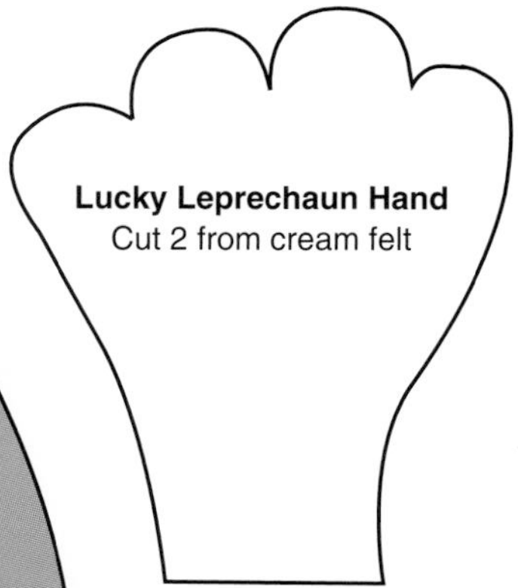

Lucky Leprechaun Hand
Cut 2 from cream felt

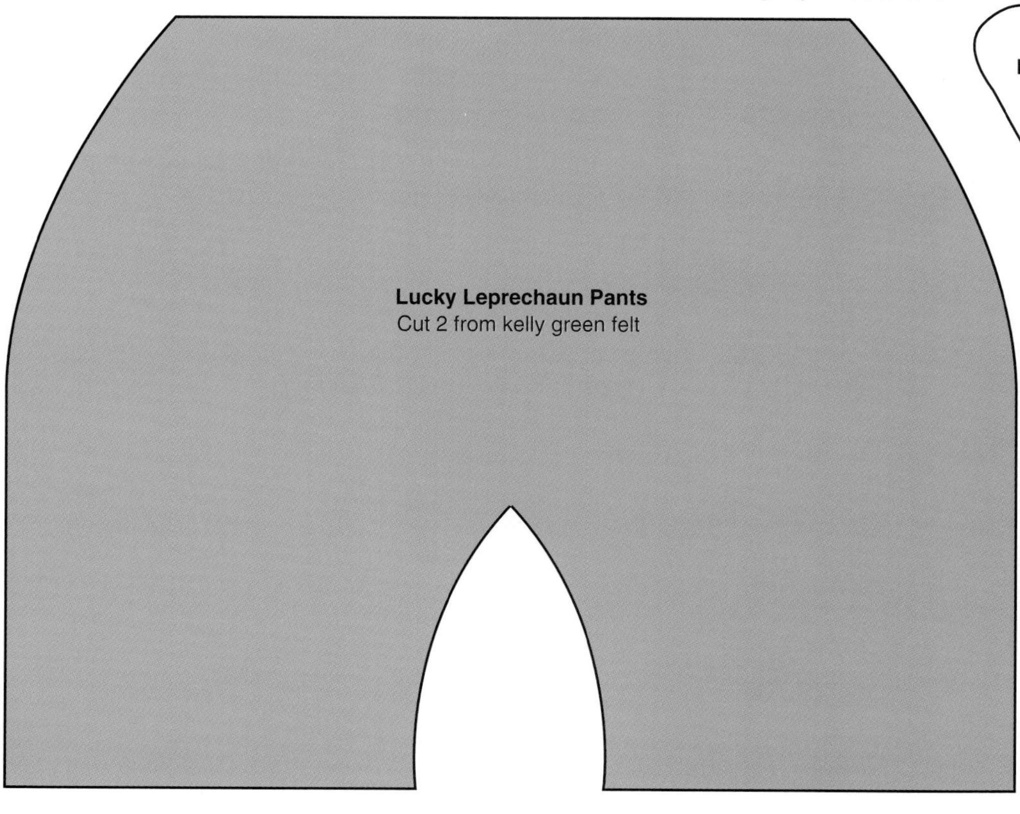

Lucky Leprechaun Pants
Cut 2 from kelly green felt

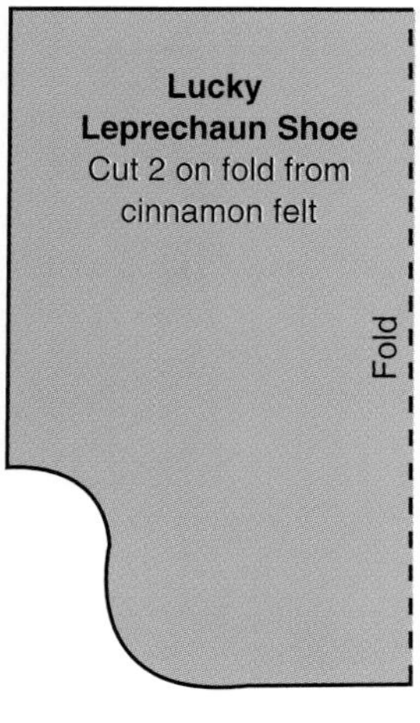

Lucky Leprechaun Shoe
Cut 2 on fold from cinnamon felt

Fold

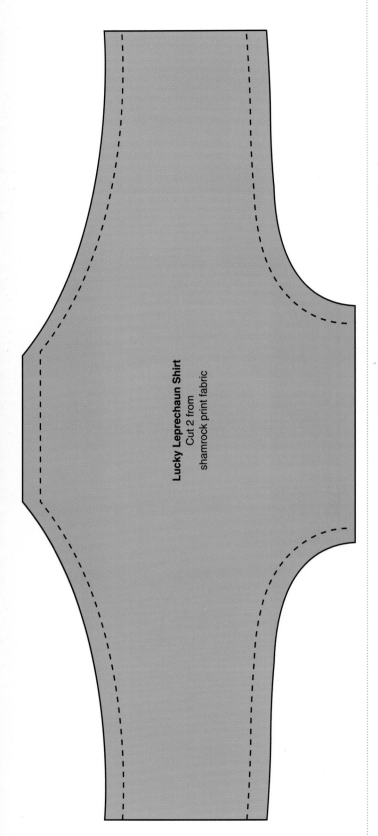

Lucky Leprechaun Shirt
Cut 2 from
shamrock print fabric

Shamrock Tree

*Straight from the pages of legend comes
this tree blooming in lucky shamrocks!
It's easy to dress up a purchased tree
with shamrocks made from fabric
in an appropriate shade of green.*

Materials
- Purchased tree
- ¼ yard green fabric
- ¼ yard iron-on adhesive
- Pressing cloth
- 9" x 15" piece of brown paper
- White marking pencil
- 3 yards fine jute twine
- 15 (⅜") marbled tan buttons
- Hot-glue gun

Instructions

1. Following manufacturer's instructions, fuse adhesive to wrong side of green fabric, covering fabric with pressing cloth. Cut fabric into two 9" x 15" pieces.

2. Remove paper backing. Lay one piece of fabric on brown paper and fuse. Lay the other piece on the other side of the paper; fuse.

3. Trace 15 or more shamrocks onto fabric with marking pencil and cut out.

4. Cut jute into 15 equal pieces. Bend each in half and glue ends to back of each shamrock near top. Glue button to center front of each shamrock. Hang shamrocks on tree. ❧

—Design by Angie Wilhite

**Shamrock
Tree Shamrock
Cut 15**

Irish Rainbow Box

Here's a lovely spot to keep your treasured lucky piece—or a wonderful presentation piece for a special gift. It stitches up quickly in plenty of bright colors.

Stitch Count
38 W x 34 H

Design Size
2⅝" W x 2⅜" H

Materials
- 5" square of bone 28-count Brittney fabric
- DMC 6-strand embroidery floss as listed in color key
- DMC metallic 6-strand embroidery floss as listed in color key
- Embroidery hoop
- #24 tapestry needle
- 2½" box with lid for cross-stitch

Instructions

1. Using 3 strands floss and metallic floss, cross-stitch design in center of fabric.

2. Using very dark gold throughout, Backstitch pot handle and rings with 3 strands. Backstitch outline of pot with 1 strand.

3. Mount fabric in lid following box manufacturer's instructions. ♣

—Design by Kathleen Marie O'Donnell

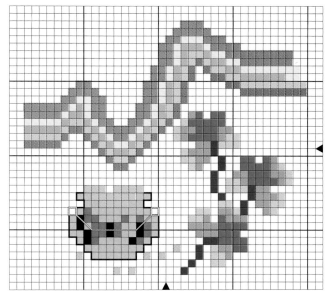

Irish Rainbow Box
38 W x 34 H

COLOR KEY
6-Strand Embroidery Floss
- ▨ Lavender #210
- ▨ Light gold #725
- ■ Dark yellow #843
- ▨ Dark gold #783
- ▨ Dark Pink #894
- ▨ Dark green #910
- ▨ Medium green #912
- ▨ Light green #954
- ■ Very dark green #986
- ☐ Pale yellow #3078
- ▨ Orange #3341
- ▨ Yellow green #3348
- ▨ Blue #3747
- ✏ Very dark gold #782 (X1) Backstitch
- ✏ Very dark gold #782 (X3) Backstitch

Metallic Embroidery Floss
- ▨ Metallic gold #5282

Color numbers given are for DMC 6-strand embroidery floss and metallic embroidery floss.

Smiling Leprechaun

*Sure, and who could be more welcome on St. Patrick's Day than your own personal leprechaun?
Here he is, wearing rosy cheeks and a smile as bright as his emerald green bow tie.*

Materials
- Craft foam sheets (1 each): green, black, orange and white
- Small piece of gold felt
- 2 (8mm) movable round eyes
- Black permanent fine-tip marker
- Powdered cosmetic blusher
- Cotton swab
- 9½" ⅜"-wide green grosgrain ribbon
- Seam sealant
- Tacky craft glue
- Craft cement
- 1½" pin back or magnet adhesive strip

Instructions

1. Trace pattern pieces onto tracing paper; cut out.

2. Using paper patterns, cut pieces from craft foam sheets and gold felt as directed.

3. Using craft glue and referring to photo through step 6, glue hatband onto hat; glue felt buckle to hatband. Let dry.

4. Glue face to beard/hair; glue hat to face. Let dry. Glue eyebrows and eyes in place.

5. With permanent marker, add facial features. Dip cotton swab into blusher; add color to cheeks.

6. Tie ribbon in bow; trim ends at an angle and apply seam sealant; let dry. Referring to photo, glue bow below leprechaun's chin.

7. Using craft cement, glue pin back to back of shamrock. Or, peel backing from adhesive magnet strip and press in place. ✤

—*Design by Helen L. Rafson*

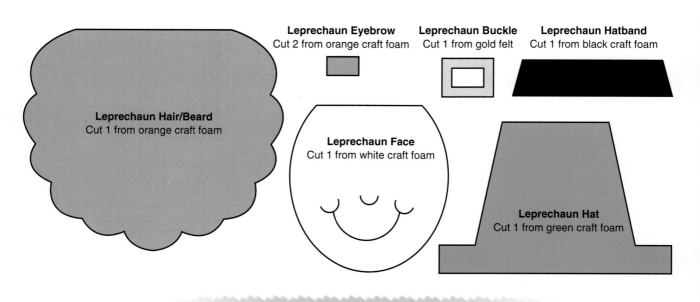

Leprechaun Hair/Beard
Cut 1 from orange craft foam

Leprechaun Eyebrow
Cut 2 from orange craft foam

Leprechaun Buckle
Cut 1 from gold felt

Leprechaun Hatband
Cut 1 from black craft foam

Leprechaun Face
Cut 1 from white craft foam

Leprechaun Hat
Cut 1 from green craft foam

Happy Shamrock

Used to be, those who dared emerge on St. Patrick's Day without a wisp of green on their persons were in for a hearty pinch or two! While green may not be everyone's color, this little fellow is fun for all to wear! Or, if you'd rather, replace the pin back with a magnet strip.

Materials

- Craft foam sheets (1 each): dark green, light green, black and white
- Small piece of gold felt
- Black permanent fine-tip marker
- Hole punch
- Auburn brown mini-curl doll hair
- 7¼" ¼"-wide green satin ribbon
- Seam sealant
- Tacky craft glue
- Craft cement
- 2 (7mm) movable round eyes
- 1½" pin back or magnet adhesive strip

Instructions

1. Trace pattern pieces onto tracing paper; cut out.

2. Using paper patterns, cut pieces from craft foam sheets and gold felt as directed.

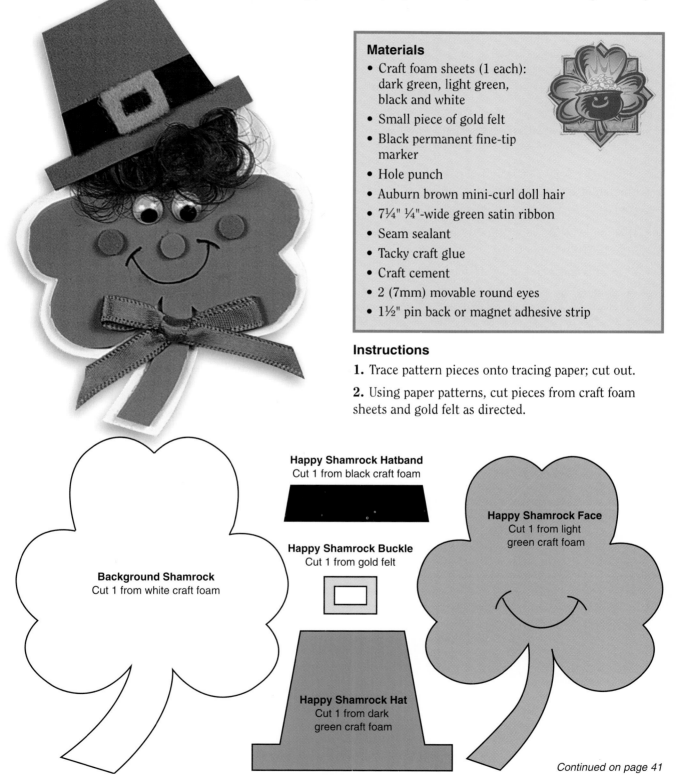

Background Shamrock
Cut 1 from white craft foam

Happy Shamrock Hatband
Cut 1 from black craft foam

Happy Shamrock Buckle
Cut 1 from gold felt

Happy Shamrock Hat
Cut 1 from dark green craft foam

Happy Shamrock Face
Cut 1 from light green craft foam

Continued on page 41

Pot o' Gold Table Set

Stitch up a set of these colorful place mats and napkin rings in a hurry, and enjoy the real treasures found around your table—the love of family and friends who gather there.

Materials

Each Place Mat

- Cotton-blend fabrics: black, gold and green
- Cream place mat
- Fusible webbing
- Sewing machine with zigzag option
- Sewing needle
- Matching sewing threads
- Emerald green baby rickrack
- 10" strip Offray's 1½"-wide Rainbow Stripe ribbon
- 10¼" ⅜"-wide green grosgrain ribbon
- Seam sealant
- 7 (16mm) and 3 (19mm) gold coin charms

Each Napkin Ring

- 1½"-wide ring cut from 1 end of a cardboard roll from bathroom tissue, paper towels, etc.
- Green acrylic paint
- Paintbrush
- 5½" strip Offray's 1½"-wide Rainbow Stripe ribbon
- 9" ⅜"-wide green grosgrain ribbon
- Seam sealant
- Tacky craft glue
- 16mm gold coin charm
- Sewing needle
- Gold thread

Place Mat

1. Preshrink cotton-blend fabrics, if necessary.

2. Trace patterns onto tracing paper; cut out.

3. Following manufacturer's instructions, fuse webbing to wrong sides of all fabrics. Trace patterns onto back of webbing; cut out as directed.

4. Referring to photo, fuse pot to place mat. Machine-appliqué with black thread.

5. Fuse gold section onto pot; machine-appliqué with matching thread.

6. Fuse green band onto pot; machine-appliqué with matching thread.

7. Stitch rickrack around border of place mat.

8. Referring to photo throughout, measure rainbow ribbon to fit from middle of gold section to top of place mat, leaving enough to turn to back of place mat. Apply seam sealant to ribbon ends; let dry. Sew ribbon in place.

9. Fuse shamrocks to place mat; machine-appliqué with matching thread.

10. Tie green ribbon in a bow, cutting ends at an angle. Apply seam sealant to cut ends; let dry. Referring to photo, stitch bow to pot. Sew gold coins in place.

Napkin Ring

1. Paint inside of cardboard ring with green paint; let dry.

2. Apply seam sealant to ends of rainbow ribbon; let dry. Glue around cardboard ring. Let dry.

3. Tie green ribbon in a bow, cutting ends at an angle. Apply seam sealant to cut ends; let dry.

4. Referring to photo, sew coin to knot of bow; glue bow to napkin ring. Let dry. ❖

—Designs by Helen L. Rafson

Cut 1 from gold

Pot o' Gold Table Set
Cut 1 pot from black;
Cut 1 pot interior from gold

Pot o' Gold Band
Cut 1 from green fabric

Pot o' Gold Shamrock
Cut 3, reversing 1
from green fabric

Happy Shamrock

Continued from page 39

3. Using craft glue and referring to photo through step 7, glue hatband onto hat; glue felt buckle to hatband.

4. Glue green shamrock to white shamrock shape. Referring to photo, draw smile with permanent marker.

5. With hole punch, punch one light green foam circle for nose and two dark green circles for cheeks. Glue in place; glue eyes in place.

6. Glue wisps of hair to top of shamrock's head; let dry. Glue hat to top of head; let dry.

7. Tie ribbon in bow; trim ends at an angle and apply seam sealant; let dry. Referring to photo, glue onto shamrock stem.

8. Using craft cement, glue pin back to back of shamrock. Or, peel backing from adhesive magnet strip and press in place. ❖

—Design by Helen L. Rafson

Shamrock Napkin Ring

Dressed up with cheerful rickrack, these easy-to-make napkin rings will lend a touch of fun to your St. Pat's Day table.

Materials

Each Napkin Ring

- 2" square of green fabric
- Fusible webbing
- 1⅝"-wide ring cut from 1 end of a cardboard roll from bathroom tissue, paper towels, etc.
- Cream acrylic paint
- Paintbrush
- Emerald green medium rickrack
- Tacky craft glue

Instructions

1. Trace shamrock and cut out. Following manufacturer's instructions, fuse webbing to back of fabric. Trace shamrock onto webbing; cut out.

2. Paint inside and outside of cardboard ring with two coats of cream paint, allowing paint to dry thoroughly between coats and after final coat.

3. Referring to photo throughout, measure and glue rickrack to fit around inside at each end of ring; let dry.

4. Glue shamrock to napkin ring; let dry. ❖

—Design by Helen L. Rafson

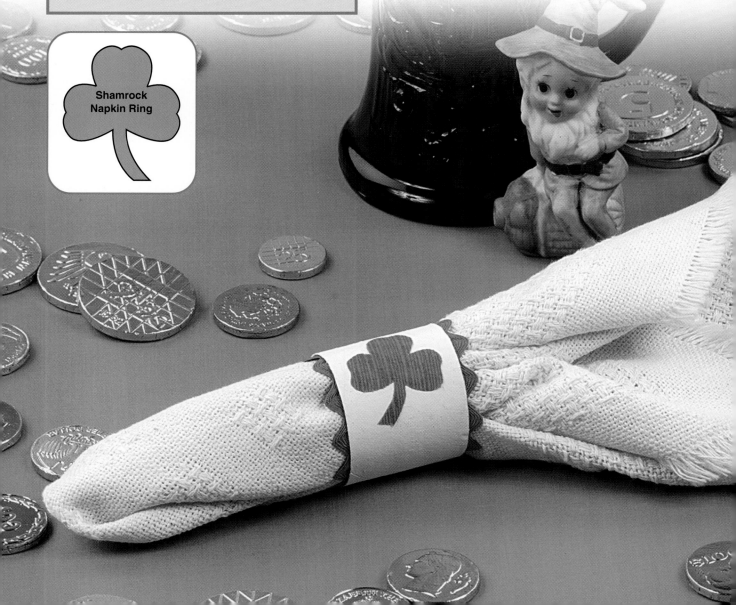

Shamrock
Napkin Ring

Gilded Shamrock Pin

Search out a few really unusual glass beads to give this pin your own unique touch. Kissed with gold, this brooch is a super gift for anyone who's proud to be Irish!

Materials
- Rusted tin from Bits & Pieces by Joan
- Aleene's Essentials: Gold #OC 301
- Aleene's Premium-Coat Acrylic paints: Deep green #OC 140
- 3 decorative glass beads
- Sandpaper
- Small stiff-bristle brush
- Hot-glue gun
- Pin back

Project Note
For best results, read all instructions before beginning.

Instructions
1. Using shamrock template, trace and cut shamrock shape from rusted tin with scissors. Sand edges smooth.

2. Paint shamrock gold; let dry. Use sandpaper to make distress marks or scratches on the painted surface.

3. Dry-brush edges of shamrock with deep green: Dip tip of stiff-bristle brush into undiluted paint. Wipe off almost all the paint onto a paper towel. Brush over the surface with little or no pressure to create a softly textured, aged look. Repeat for more opaque coverage. Do not use water on the brush until you have finished layering on the paint.

4. Glue glass beads in center; let dry. Glue pin back to back. ♣

—Design by Jennifer Blevins for Duncan Enterprises

Shamrock Template

Beaded Shamrock Pin

Here's a lovely little touch of green, guaranteed to bring you the luck of the Irish!

Materials
- 1 sheet white perforated paper
- #9 quilting needle
- 1 skein white 6-strand embroidery floss
- Mill Hill Products seed beads from Gay Bowles Sales Inc. as listed in color key
- 4" square Pellon fusible interfacing
- Pin back

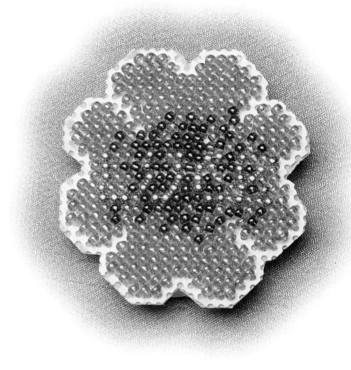

Project Note

For basic information on beading, refer to the Project Notes that accompany instructions for the Beaded Heart Pin (page 31).

Instructions

1. Cut a 4" square of perforated paper. Identify paper's right side; it is the smoother side. Find center of square; mark lightly on *wrong* side with pencil. Count up and to the left to find end of top row where first bead will be attached; mark on wrong side.

2. Cut 18" length of embroidery floss; separate into individual strands. Thread 1 strand onto needle.

3. Attach beads as shown on graph.

4. When all beads are attached, iron fusible interfacing onto back of design: Lay thick terry towel on ironing board. Place beaded piece right side down on towel; lay dot side of fusible interfacing atop wrong side of beading. Iron in place.

5. With small scissors, trim away excess paper and fusible interfacing, leaving a margin of at least one row of unworked paper around design.

6. Sew pin back onto back of design, taking care not to tear paper. ❧

—Design by Rhonda Semonis

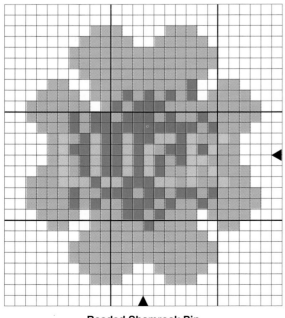

Beaded Shamrock Pin
22 beads x 24 beads

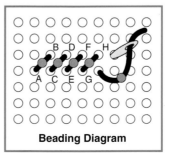

Beading Diagram

COLOR KEY	
Beads	**Packets**
Green #157	2
Dark green #332	1
Gold #557	1
Color numbers given are for Mill Hill seed beads.	

Shamrock Button Covers

Add a touch of emerald to a button-up blouse with these simple, quick button covers.

Materials

- 2 (2¼" x 12") pieces fusible webbing
- 2¼" x 12" green fabric
- 2¼" x 12" green felt
- 24" each of 3 coordinating shades of green ¾"-wide grosgrain ribbon
- 5 button covers
- Thick tacky craft glue
- Gold glitter dimensional paint
- Straight pins

Shamrock Button Covers Pattern

Instructions

1. Read manufacturer's instructions for using fusible webbing. Position textured side of web against green fabric for backing. Transfer the glue and peel off paper backing. Place fusible side down on felt and iron.

2. Turn felt over to transfer fusible web to the other side of the felt. Position textured side of web against felt. Transfer the glue and peel off the paper backing.

3. Cut each shade of ribbon in half, making six 12" pieces. Pin one of each shade to the felt, side by side; repeat the color pattern. Iron to transfer ribbons to felt.

4. Trace shamrock pattern onto paper and cut out. Place paper pattern on ribbons, positioning so that ribbon rows run horizontally or vertically. Trace five shamrocks onto ribbon, varying placement so different color patterns run through shamrocks. Cut out.

5. Outline each shamrock with dimensional paint. Let dry flat for 24 hours.

6. Glue button covers to backs of shamrocks. ♣

—Design by Ellen Douglas

Easter Fun & Surprises

Celebrate the arrival of spring with cheerful Easter gifts, decorations and party favors! This chapter brings you more than a dozen projects for crafting whimsical bunnies, adorable chicks and colorful eggs, sure to make this holiday extra-special and extra-fun!

Bunny Wishes

Stitch a bunny bearing a sweet message for someone dear.
Tuck miniature items in her pocket, or a slip of paper with a funny poem,
prayer, chore coupon or special wish for a special day.

Materials

- 8" x 16" piece light-value fabric (A)
- 6" x 12" piece dark-value fabric (B)
- Small piece of peach fabric
- Fusible transfer webbing
- Sewing thread to coordinate with Fabric A
- Rayon thread to contrast with Fabric B
- Pinking shears (optional)
- Fine-point permanent black marking pen
- Polyester fiberfill
- Assorted embellishments: miniature basket, straw hat, ribbons, silk or dried flowers, etc.
- Craft glue and/or glue gun

Instructions

1. Fold Fabric B wrong sides facing. Referring to patterns, cut two pairs ears from doubled fabric, using pinking shears if desired. Also from Fabric B, cut one 2¼" x 12" strip.

2. Fold Fabric A wrong sides facing. Cut one pair of body pieces from doubled fabric, using pinking shears if desired.

3. Place adhesive side of fusible webbing

on wrong side of peach fabric and remainder of Fabric B; fuse, following manufacturer's instructions. Trace face and hands onto paper backing of peach, and sleeves on paper backing of Fabric B. Cut out; peel off paper.

4. Referring to photo (page 46) throughout, position face and arms on front of body; tuck hands under sleeves. Fuse all pieces.

5. Thread upper part of sewing machine with rayon thread; place bobbin of sewing thread in bottom. Machine-appliqué around face, hands and sleeves with close zigzag stitch.

6. Turn under one long edge of 2½" x 12" strip to make narrow hem; zigzag by machine. Place

Continued on page 56

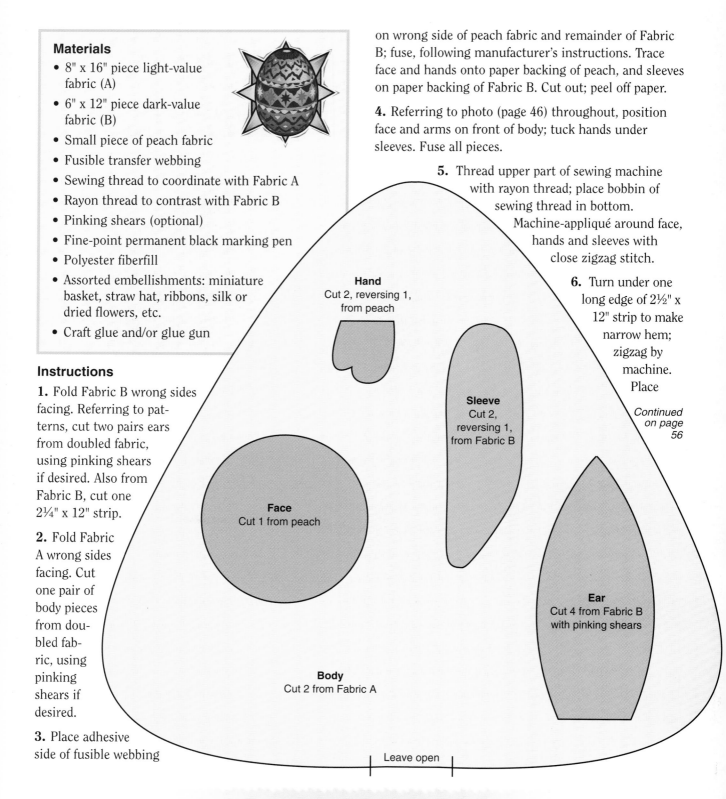

Hand
Cut 2, reversing 1, from peach

Sleeve
Cut 2, reversing 1, from Fabric B

Face
Cut 1 from peach

Ear
Cut 4 from Fabric B with pinking shears

Body
Cut 2 from Fabric A

Leave open

Mr. & Mrs. Bunny Spools

These cuties are too sweet to pass up! Make a bunch to use for table decorations and charming additions to Easter baskets. Secure a wooden skewer inside with a dab of glue or florist's clay and add them as plant pokes to those Easter gift arrangements.

Materials

- 2 large empty spools
- Pink felt
- White felt
- White craft foam sheet
- 6 (2") pieces gray 6-strand embroidery floss
- Seam sealant
- 4 (8mm) round black movable eyes
- 2 (7mm) pink pompons
- 4 (¼") white pompons
- Craft glue
- 7½" ¼"-wide light blue ribbon
- 7½" ⅛"-wide white ribbon
- 3¾" ⅜"-wide white crocheted edging
- 4½" ⅛" white pearls by the yard

Instructions

1. Remove all labels from spools.

2. Trace inner ears and teeth onto felt; cut out. Cut out two 1⅛" circles from white felt. Trace outer ears onto white craft foam; cut out.

3. Referring to photo throughout, glue inner ear to center of each outer ear. Glue felt circle to top of each spool; glue ears to tops of felt circles and let dry.

4. Glue eyes in place, and embroidery floss strands for whiskers; glue teeth in place.

5. Glue on pink pompon noses and white pompons for cheeks.

6. Tie light blue ribbon in bow; trim ends at an angle and coat with seam sealant. Glue bow to Mr. Bunny's chin.

7. Glue crochet trim, then white pearls by the yard around base of Mrs. Bunny's neck; tie white ribbon in bow and glue in place. ●

—*Designs by Helen L. Rafson*

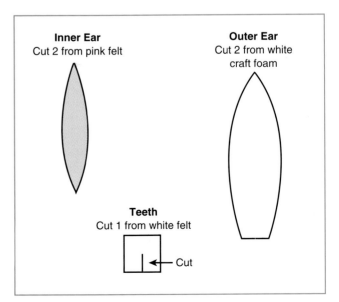

Inner Ear
Cut 2 from pink felt

Outer Ear
Cut 2 from white craft foam

Teeth
Cut 1 from white felt

← Cut

Easter Egg Tree

*Here's a terrific centerpiece for your Easter table,
painted in bright springtime pastels and loaded with eggs!*

Materials

- Aleene's Enhancers:
  All-Purpose Primer #EN 104
  Matte Varnish #EN 107
- Aleene's Premium-Coat Acrylic paints:
  Light yellow #OC 125
  Light green #OC 137
  Light turquoise #OC 143
  Light lavender #OC 155
  Light fuchsia #OC 167
  White #OC 173
- ¾" flat brush
- #10/0 liner brush
- #10 flat brush
- Spatter brush
- Tacky craft glue
- Drill
- Fabric scraps in various springtime plaids and prints
- 2 stems white florist wire
- White poster board
- Sandpaper
- Utility sponge
- 19" ½"-diameter dowel
- 25" ¼"-diameter wooden dowels
- 11 wooden eggs
- 10"-wide 1"-thick wooden heart base
- 6"-diameter ¾"-thick wooden circle
- 4"-diameter ½"-thick wooden circle

Project Notes

Read all instructions before beginning. Refer to photo (page 51) throughout.

For this project, a "plop" is made as follows:
Using fully loaded tip of round or liner brush, touch surface at 45-degree angle, then remove brush, leaving a "plop" of color.

Instructions

1. Mix equal parts primer and water. Using ¾" flat brush, apply to all wood surfaces. Let dry. Sand.

2. Using ¾" flat brush, base-coat tops and bottoms of heart and circles as follows: heart—light lavender; 6" circle—light fuchsia; 4" circle—light turquoise. Paint sides of heart and circles and ¼" dowel light yellow. Paint ½" dowel light green.

3. Thin white paint with water to the consistency of ink. Using #10/0 liner brush, paint lifeline (wavy line representing life's ups and downs) around top edge of heart and both circles. Spatter each piece lightly with white, using spatter brush.

4. Using ¾" flat brush, base-coat eggs. Use white for at least one of the eggs; set aside for the bunny, which will top the tree. Paint others light fuchsia, light yellow, light turquoise, light green and light lavender. Let dry.

5. Add painted patterns and decorations of your choice to pastel eggs. A few suggestions include:

- Using #10 flat brush and white, paint broad stripes around top, bottom and center of a light yellow egg. Using #10/0 liner brush, paint light turquoise zigzags between white stripes. Paint small plops of light fuchsia around center of middle white stripe.

- Using sponge, lightly sponge light fuchsia over light turquoise egg; let dry. With liner brush, add curlicues and bull's-eye designs randomly over surface in light yellow and light green.

- Using #10 flat brush, paint four light fuchsia roses around center of a light lavender egg. Using liner, plop white in center top of each. Using liner, paint three light green leaves on each rose. Add light yellow zigzags around top and bottom.

6. *Bunny egg:* Cut 2" ears from poster board; using ¾" flat brush, paint ears white. Using permanent marker, add eyes and nose to egg. Side-load #10 flat brush with light fuchsia; paint cheeks and insides of ears.

7. Apply one or two protective coats of matte varnish to eggs with ¾" flat brush.

8. Drill ½" hole in base and through center of each circle. Drill six ¼" holes ½" deep evenly spaced around edge of 6" circle, and four ¼"holes ½" deep and evenly spaced around edge of 4" circle. Drill ¼" hole ½" deep into sides of pastel eggs, and ½" hole ½" deep into bottom of bunny egg.

9. Insert ½" dowel into heart base; slide on 6" and 4" circles, spacing evenly and gluing to secure. Cut ¼" dowel into 2½" sections; insert one into each pastel egg; glue. Insert other end into holes in sides of circles, balancing colors in a pleasing arrangement.

10. Curl florist wire around wooden brush handle to make whiskers for bunny egg. Drill two tiny holes on each side of nose; insert whiskers and glue in place. Glue ears to top of bunny; cut small fabric strip and tie in bow; glue atop bunny's head. Place bunny egg onto top of ½" dowel; glue to secure.

11. Cut fabrics into strips; tie one into bow at top of center dowel, under the bunny on both sides, and at base of center dowel. Tie two strips onto each short dowel connecting egg to tree. ●

—*Design by Bonnie Stephens*
for Duncan Enterprises

Punch-Dot Bunnies Table Set

Colorful craft foam and a simple hole punch are the basic materials needed to create this cute set of decorations for your Easter table. The charming basket with decorated eggs, bunny candy cups and napkin rings will delight Easter diners of all ages!

Materials

Basket & Eggs

- 8"-diameter natural vine basket
- Darice Foamies craft foam sheets: white, pink, purple, green, blue, yellow, brown, red
- Large paper punch (¼")
- 5 (2⅜") plastic foam eggs
- Small piece of plastic foam
- Craft glue
- Toothpicks
- White acrylic craft paint
- Excelsior: natural, green and pink

Candy Cup

- Darice Foamies craft foam sheets: white, pink, purple, blue, yellow, brown, red

- Large paper punch (¼" circles)
- Craft glue
- Toothpicks
- White acrylic craft paint
- Disposable 2" white plastic drinking cup
- Small amount of pink excelsior

Napkin Ring

- Darice Foamies craft foam sheets: white, pink, purple, green, yellow, brown, red
- Large paper punch (¼" circles)
- Craft glue
- Toothpicks
- White acrylic craft paint
- Disposable 2" white plastic drinking cup

Instructions

Basket & Eggs

1. Referring to patterns (page 54), trace and cut two basket bunny heads, two straight ears, two floppy ears and one bunny body, all from white; four inner ears, four eyes, one tummy and one tail, all from pink; and one collar from purple.

2. Using paper punch, punch four brown dots, two red dots and three yellow dots.

3. *Assemble standing bunny:* Referring to photo throughout and using a toothpick to apply tiny amounts of glue, glue collar to top of body; glue head atop collar. Glue one straight ear and one floppy ear to back of head. Glue two inner ears, two eyes and tummy in place.

4. Glue two brown dots onto eyes for pupils; glue one red dot to face for nose; glue yellow dots down tummy for buttons.

5. Using white paint and toothpick, paint a tiny eye highlight in each pupil; let dry.

6. From green foam, cut one 3" x ¹⁄₁₆" strip; tie into a small bow and glue below bunny's chin and over collar.

Glue tail to back of bunny.

7. *Assemble bunny head for top of basket:* Glue remaining ears to back of head; glue eyes and inner ears in place. Glue on brown pupils and red nose.

8. Using white paint and toothpick, paint a tiny eye highlight in each pupil; let dry.

9. *Eggs:* "Sand" eggs lightly with the small piece of plastic foam to make a smooth surface.

10. Punch 12 or more dots each from green, yellow, purple, blue and pink foam sheets. Glue dots of one color to surface of each egg.

11. *Basket:* Place natural excelsior in bottom of basket; top with small amounts of pink and green excelsior.

12. Stand standing bunny in excelsior on left side of basket; apply a tiny amount of glue to backs of ears and glue to handle to hold him in place. Glue bunny head to top center of handle.

13. Cut several 4" x ¹⁄₁₆" strips from various colors of craft foam; tie around twigs at top of basket. Place decorated eggs in basket.

Continued on page 54

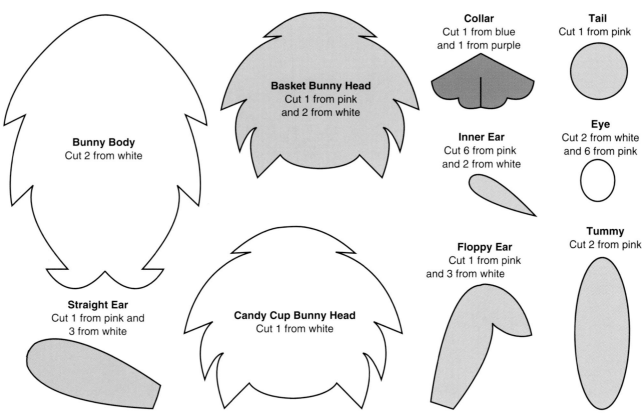

Collar
Cut 1 from blue
and 1 from purple

Tail
Cut 1 from pink

Basket Bunny Head
Cut 1 from pink
and 2 from white

Inner Ear
Cut 6 from pink
and 2 from white

Eye
Cut 2 from white
and 6 from pink

Bunny Body
Cut 2 from white

Tummy
Cut 2 from pink

Floppy Ear
Cut 1 from pink
and 3 from white

Candy Cup Bunny Head
Cut 1 from white

Straight Ear
Cut 1 from pink and
3 from white

Candy Cup

1. Referring to patterns (above), trace and cut one candy cup bunny head, one straight ear, one floppy ear and one bunny body, all from white; two inner ears, two eyes and one tummy, all from pink; and one collar from blue.

2. Using paper punch, punch two brown dots, one red dot and three purple dots.

3. Referring to photo throughout and using a toothpick to apply tiny amounts of glue, glue collar and tummy to body. Glue purple dots down tummy for buttons. From yellow foam, cut one 3" x 1/16" strip; tie into a small bow and glue to top of collar.

4. Glue ears to back of head; glue inner ears and eyes in place. Glue brown dots onto eyes for pupils; glue red dot to face for nose. Using white paint and toothpick, paint a tiny eye highlight in each pupil; let dry.

5. Set cup on work surface. Glue body to front of cup so feet rest on work surface; glue head to back of cup. Let dry.

6. Place pink excelsior in cup; add jelly beans or other candies.

Napkin Ring

1. Referring to patterns (above), trace and cut one basket

bunny head, one straight ear and one floppy ear, all from pink; and two inner ears and two eyes, all from white.

2. Using paper punch, punch two brown dots, one red, and eight to 10 other dots in assorted colors.

3. Referring to photo throughout and using a toothpick to apply tiny amounts of glue, glue ears to back of head; glue inner ears and eyes in place. Glue brown dots onto eyes for pupils; glue red dot to face for nose. From purple foam, cut one 3" x 1/16" strip; tie into a small bow and glue to bottom of head.

4. Using white paint and toothpick, paint a tiny eye highlight in each pupil; let dry.

5. Trim bottom from disposable plastic cup as shown in Fig. 1. Glue bunny head to cup with ears extending above cutout end. Glue dots in assorted colors over surface of cup. Slide napkin through openings in cup. ●

–Designs by Joanna Randolph Rott

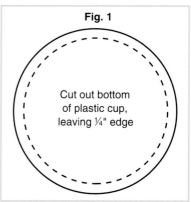

Fig. 1

Cut out bottom
of plastic cup,
leaving 1/4" edge

Keepsake Eggs

Turn real eggs into heirloom-quality treasures with delightful trims of ribbon, lace, beads, buttons and silk flowers.

Materials

- Large needle
- Real egg
- Matte-finish spray paint
- 4 large pearl beads
- Craft glue
- Scraps of ribbon, gathered lace
- Various dried and/or silk flowers, foliage, eucalyptus leaves, etc.
- Assorted beads, pearls, buttons, etc.

Instructions

1. Choose a fresh egg with no cracks or blemishes. With large needle, carefully pierce small end. Stick needle down into egg and twirl to break yolk. Pierce slightly larger hole in large end. Blow out contents of egg from small end through large end. Set aside to dry.

2. Spray-paint egg in desired color. Allow to dry.

3. Position four large pearl beads on one side of egg and glue in place for feet.

4. Referring to photo throughout, glue ribbon around egg to conceal holes in ends.

5. Glue gathered lace to top of egg. Embellish with glued-on silk or dried blossoms, leaves, etc. Top with a ribbon bow and a few pearl beads, if desired.

–Design by Louy Danube

Felt Bunny Pin

*Precut wooden pieces make this cute pin
a snap to construct! The kids will enjoy
helping you make these, too.*

Materials

- 6" sheet Coats Instant Stick &
  Hold craft adhesive
- 2" square pink felt
- 4" square white felt
- Forster Woodsies wooden
  shapes:
  1"-wide wooden heart
  1⅝"-wide wooden heart
  2 (1½"-wide) wooden teardrops
- 2 (6mm) round black moveable eyes
- 5" ⅛"-wide pink ribbon
- ¾" pin back
- Fine-point black permanent fabric pen
- Cotton swab
- Cosmetic powder blusher
- Hot-glue gun

Instructions

1. Cut 4" and 2" squares from adhesive sheet. Remove
paper backing. Press 4" square onto back of white felt
and 2" square onto back of pink felt.

2. Trace larger heart and two teardrop shapes on paper
side of white felt. Trace small heart onto paper side of
pink felt. Cut out pieces.

3. Remove paper backing from felt; press onto backs of
corresponding wooden pieces.

4. Referring to photo throughout, glue ears to back of
bunny head; glue pink heart to center of white heart.
Glue eyes to pink heart.

5. Tie ribbon in small bow; trim ends as needed. Glue to
white heart. Glue pin back to back of bunny.

6. Draw mouth with black pen. Using cotton swab, add
cheeks with powder blusher. ●

—Design by Angie Wilhite

Bunny Wishes

Continued from page 48

strip right side up along bottom front of bunny, hem at
top. Zigzag strip to bunny front, attaching with vertical
rows of stitching to make four pockets.

7. Set machine for straight stitch, 15–16 stitches per
inch. Stitch each pair of ears together, wrong sides facing, stitching ¼" from edge. Pin front and back of
bunny together wrong sides facing, in-
serting ears at top. Stitch bunny halves
together, stitching ¼" from edge and
leaving bottom opening for stuffing. Trim
edges of pocket strip at bottom even with
body edges. Clip edges of bunny body and

ears at even intervals up to but not through stitching.

8. Stuff bunny firmly with stuffing; close opening by
machine. Draw facial features on peach face circle with
marking pen, referring to face diagrams.

9. Embellish finished bunny as desired with miniature
hat, basket, ribbons, strips of fabric tied in bows, silk or
dried flowers, etc. Tuck messages or goodies in pockets. ●

—Design by Beth Wheeler

Bunny Wishes Faces

Easter Party Favors

Give an irresistible touch of springtime charm to your table with these colorful flowerpots.

Materials

Each Favor

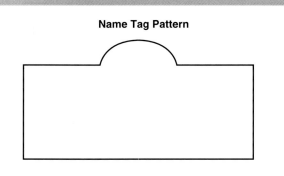

- Small piece white cardboard or poster board
- Black marking pen
- Dimensional craft paint
- Craft stick
- 2⅞"-wide terra cotta flowerpot with 4½" saucer
- Colorful shredded paper
- Small flying creature on wire: ladybug, dragon fly, butterfly, etc.
- Small wooden ornaments: bunny, carrot, birdhouse, etc.
- 3 small silk blossoms
- Jelly beans or candy eggs
- Craft glue and/or glue gun
- Craft cement

Name Tag Pattern

Instructions

1. For each favor, cut a name tag from white cardboard or poster board. Write name on tag with marking pen. Referring to photo throughout, outline name tag with dimensional craft paint; set aside to dry completely.

When dry, glue name tag to end of craft stick.

2. Stuff pot firmly with shredded paper. Apply glue to other end of craft stick; insert into shredded paper.

3. Coil wire attached to flying creature around pencil, leaving end straight. Apply glue to wire end; insert into shredded paper in pot.

4. With craft cement, secure flowerpot to saucer. Glue wooden bunny or other ornament so that it stands in saucer. Glue a silk blossom on each side of ornament, and another to base of name tag. Scatter jelly beans around saucer and pot and on table.

—*Design by Beth Wheeler*

Easter Napkin Rings

*Make a whole basketful of bunnies, chickabiddies and ducks—for napkin rings,
Easter egg cups, or as holders for tiny bags of jelly beans. You needn't restrict
them to Easter; they're lots of fun through the whole spring season!*

Materials

Rabbit Napkin Ring
- Cardboard tube from paper towels or bathroom tissue
- Pink felt
- White felt
- White acrylic paint
- Paintbrush
- 3 (3") pieces black 6-strand embroidery floss
- Seam sealant
- 2 (10mm) round black movable eyes
- 2 (½") white pompons
- ¼" pink pompon
- Tape
- Craft glue

Chick Napkin Ring
- Cardboard tube from paper towels or bathroom tissue
- Yellow acrylic paint
- Paintbrush
- Yellow felt
- Orange felt
- 2 (6mm) black beads
- Paper edgers with pinking blade
- Tape
- Craft glue
- 6" ⅛"-wide white ribbon

Duck Napkin Ring
- Cardboard tube from paper towels or bathroom tissue
- White acrylic paint
- Paintbrush
- White felt
- Orange felt
- 2 (6mm) black beads
- Paper edgers with pinking blade
- Tape
- Craft glue
- 6" ⅛"-wide light blue ribbon

Instructions

Rabbit Napkin Ring

1. Trace inner ears onto pink felt and teeth onto white felt; cut out. Tape body pattern around bottom of cardboard tube; trace around pattern; cut rabbit body from tube.

2. Paint rabbit body inside and out with two coats of white paint, allowing paint to dry between coats.

3. Apply seam sealant to lengths of embroidery floss to stiffen them; set aside to dry.

4. Referring to photograph throughout, glue on pink felt inner ears; glue eyes in place; glue on embroidery floss strands for whiskers. Glue on felt teeth along top edge only. Glue pink pompon in place for nose and white pompons for cheeks. Let dry.

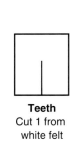

Teeth
Cut 1 from
white felt

Rabbit Pattern

Inner Ear
Cut 2 from
pink felt

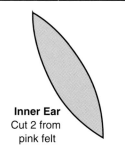

Duck Napkin Ring

1. Trace wings and bill onto felt; cut out. Tape body pattern around bottom of cardboard tube; trace around pattern; cut duck body from tube. Trim bottom of body with paper edgers.

2. Paint duck body inside and out with two coats of white paint, allowing paint to dry between coats.

3. Referring to photograph throughout, glue bead eyes and felt bill and wings in place, attaching bill only along fold and wings only along front straight edges. Let dry.

4. Tie ribbon in bow; trim ends at an angle. Glue in place.

Duck Body

Duck Wing
Cut 2 from
white felt

Duck Bill
Cut 1 from
orange felt
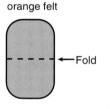
←—Fold

Chick Napkin Ring

1. Trace wings and beak onto felt; cut out. Tape body pattern around bottom of cardboard tube; trace around pattern; cut chick body from tube. Trim bottom of body with paper edgers.

2. Paint chick body inside and out with two coats of yellow paint, allowing paint to dry between coats.

3. Referring to photograph throughout, glue bead eyes and felt beak and wings in place, attaching beak only along fold and wings only along front straight edges. Let dry.

4. Tie ribbon in bow; trim ends at an angle. Glue in place. ●

—Designs by Helen L. Rafson

Chick Body

Chick Wing
Cut 2 from
yellow felt

Chick Beak
Cut 1 from
orange felt
←—Fold

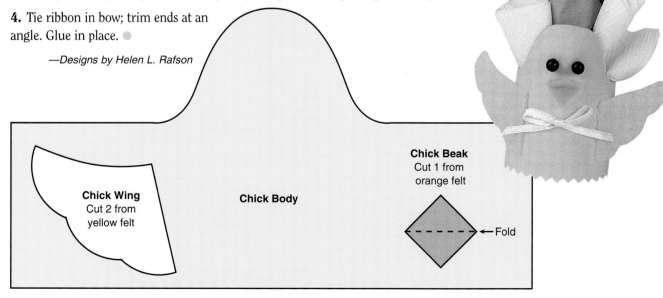

Lacy Egg 'n' Chick

*Celebrate springtime with this colorful decoration featuring
a fluffy chick and a unique "egg" of lace. Use plastic foam egg halves
as forms, drape with lace treated with fabric stiffener, and voila!*

Materials

- 1½" white plastic foam ball
- 2" white plastic foam ball
- 5⅞" x 3⅞" plastic foam egg
- 3¾" x 3" x ⅞" piece plastic foam
- Ceramcoat acrylic paints by Delta Technical Coatings: yellow, kelly green, white glitter and white pearl
- Thick craft glue
- Paintbrush
- Serrated knife
- Plastic wrap
- 2 twist ties
- Straight pins
- Liquid fabric stiffener
- Curly doll hair: white and yellow
- 1 yard 1"-wide scalloped white lace
- ⅓ yard white lace fabric
- ⅓ yard ½"-wide green satin picot-edge ribbon
- ½ yard ¼"-wide yellow satin ribbon
- ¼ yard ⅛"-wide peach satin ribbon
- Hot-glue gun
- 3 yellow feathers
- 3 round toothpicks
- Lightweight sandpaper
- 12 (¾") peach silk flowers with leaves
- 5 (¾") yellow silk flowers
- 2 (⅛") round black beads
- Scrap of orange felt

Instructions

1. Using serrated knife, carefully cut egg in half lengthwise. Tear off two generous lengths of plastic wrap; wrap one around each half, pulling plastic smoothly over curved portion of egg and gathering excess to flat side. Secure excess plastic wrap with twist tie.

2. Using sandpaper, lightly sand all sides of remaining plastic foam pieces. Referring to Fig. 1, cut slice off side of each ball. Break one toothpick in half; insert halfway into center of flat edge of large ball; press flat edge of small ball onto other end (Fig. 2).

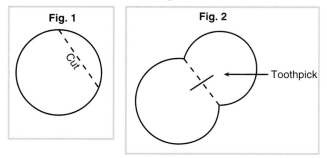

3. Place toothpick in bottom of large ball (chick body) to use as a handle while painting chick. Paint entire chick with one generous coat of yellow paint; stick toothpick into a scrap piece of craft foam to hold chick while it dries.

4. Brush top and edges of rectangular base with generous coat of green paint. Let dry completely.

5. Beginning at center of one short end of base, glue green picot-edge ribbon around bottom edge of painted base so bottom of ribbon is flush with bottom of base.

6. Glue scalloped lace around edge of base so that edges of scallops just meet top of green ribbon. Neatly fold excess scalloped ribbon onto top of base; glue in place.

7. Cut lace fabric in half (Fig. 3). Following manufacturer's instructions, pour liquid fabric stiffener into bowl; add a few drops of water. Soak lace fabric in solution for two to three minutes. Gently squeeze out excess liquid.

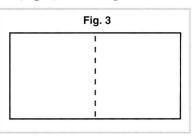

8. Drape a piece of lace fabric over rounded side of egg half, smoothing it with your fingers so that there are no pleats or tucks. Pull excess fabric to flat side of egg; pin tightly to hold lace fabric in place. Repeat with remaining fabric and egg half. Allow to dry overnight, or until fabric is completely dry and stiff.

9. Remove pins. Cut away excess lace from flat side of each egg half (Fig. 4).

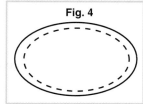

10. Using craft glue through step 11, run a generous "worm" of glue along edge of one lace egg half; allow to set for three to five minutes. Press other half of egg in place; let dry thoroughly.

11. Glue scalloped ribbon neatly over seam around lace egg.

12. Tie 2" bow with yellow ribbon, leaving long streamers. Using glue gun through step 13 and referring to photo throughout, attach bow to top of egg (over scalloped lace along seam). Glue yellow flowers and four peach flowers onto egg around bow. Tack streamers in place on egg as desired.

13. Glue egg onto base with a generous amount of glue.

14. "Knead" a small handful of yellow curly hair between fingers to soften. Holding toothpick in bottom of chick, coat painted surface of chick with craft glue. Press hair into glue; let dry. Trim hair to shape chick.

15. Cut 1"–2" ends from yellow feathers; glue ends of feathers to back of chick for tail.

16. Glue black beads to head for eyes.

17. Cut beak (Fig. 5) from orange felt; fold and glue to chick below eyes.

18. Tie small bow with peach ribbon; glue to chick's neck.

19. Use toothpick to attach right side of chick to left edge of base.

20. Place small amount of green paint in a dish; add a few drops water. Mix. Knead a large handful of white curly hair between fingers to soften. Place hair in paint; mix with fingers until hair is green. Let dry completely.

21. Apply a generous amount of craft glue to exposed areas on top of rectangular base, around chick and at base of chick. Press green curly hair into glue. Glue on remaining silk flowers. Set aside to dry completely.

22. Brush one coat white pearl paint over ribbons, silk flowers and leaves; let dry. Brush one coat glitter paint over lace egg, ribbons, flowers and leaves; let dry. ●

—Design by Joanna Randolph Rott

Easter Bunny's Day Off Garden Gloves

Decorate inexpensive garden gloves for someone you know who has a green thumb—our thumbs have green hearts!

Materials

- 2 (5" x 7") pieces apple green felt
- Scraps of hot pink and white felt
- 2 (5" x 7") pieces plus small pieces of Coats Instant Stick & Hold for Fabric craft adhesive
- 2 carrot buttons from JHB International
- Watering can, garden shears and 4 garden tool charms from JHB International
- 2 (5") pieces gold chain
- Canvas garden gloves
- Gold sewing thread and needle
- Black fine-point permanent fabric marker

Instructions

1. Fuse craft adhesive to back of felt; do not remove paper backing. Referring to patterns, trace rabbits, hearts, teeth and cheeks on back of adhesive.

2. Following manufacturer's instructions and referring to photo throughout, fuse cheeks and teeth to each rabbit; fuse a heart to front of each glove's thumb.

3. Sew chains to rabbits' hands. Sew charms and carrot buttons to chains.

4. With fine-point marker, add two small dots to each rabbit for eyes. ●

—*Design by Judi Kauffman*

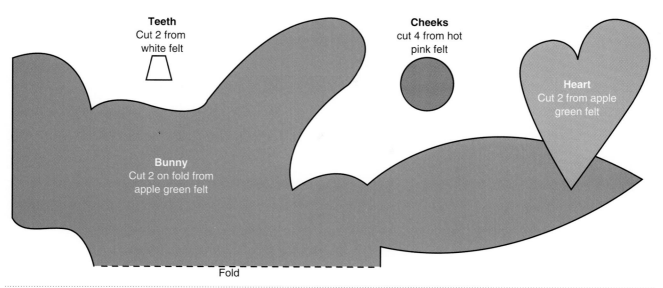

Teeth
Cut 2 from
white felt

Cheeks
cut 4 from hot
pink felt

Heart
Cut 2 from apple
green felt

Bunny
Cut 2 on fold from
apple green felt

Fold

Springtime Ornament

Finding a pretty little something to dress up those out-of-the-way spots can be a real challenge—but they add such warmth and personality to the decor! Here's the perfect solution. Play with the colors and dried materials to make it perfect for your home!

Materials

- 3½" heart-shaped grapevine wreath
- 1½" pink mushroom bird
- Small amount of Spanish moss
- 3 tiny dried rosebuds
- Tiny bunch of white dried flowers, such as pearly everlastings
- 9" ⅛"-wide dark pink satin ribbon
- 9" 1⁄16"-wide light pink satin ribbon
- 9" 1⁄16"-wide white satin ribbon
- 12" ¼"-wide picot-edge light pink satin ribbon
- Hot-glue gun
- Toothpick

Instructions

1. Referring to photo throughout, glue small bunch of Spanish moss to top right of heart wreath. Glue bird to moss and wreath.

2. Break white flowers off into very small bunches; glue below and around bird. Apply glue to stems of rosebuds; push each rosebud into moss nest so each points out from center in a different direction.

3. Tie each 9" length of ribbon into a simple bow. Apply dot of glue to center (knot) and glue to nest, using toothpick to push ribbon into the nest. To balance arrangement, glue two bows to side of nest where one rosebud is attached, and one bow to side with two rosebuds. Trim ends of ribbon at an angle.

4. Tie picot-edge ribbon to each side of wreath near top for hanging loop; leave 1½" ribbon tails. Trim ends at an angle.

—Design by Christine Malone

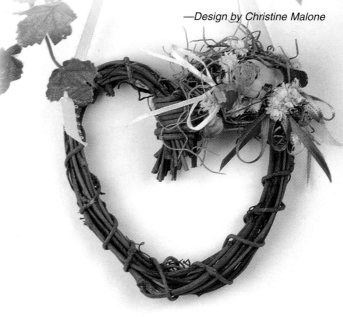

I
LOVE
you
DAD

Just for Mom & Dad

Tell Mom and Dad "I love you" in a special way this year by creating several of the attractive gift ideas included in this chapter. Watch Mom's face light up as she opens a lovely candy floral arrangement or colorful memory album. And Dad will feel like the world's luckiest father when he sees a handy note holder or Southwestern desk organizers!

Papa Bear Notepad Holder

The "papa bear" in your family "den" will appreciate a cute and thoughtful accessory for holding those convenient adhesive notes.

Materials

- 8½" x 5¾" corrugated cardboard from box, etc.
- 20" piece 20-gauge black wire
- 4 (30") strands natural raffia
- Felt: sage green, tan, cinnamon, brown and cranberry red
- Tacky craft glue
- Black slick dimensional paint
- 2" x 3" pad of adhesive notes
- Craft knife

Instructions

1. Trace bear outline in center of clean side of cardboard; without cutting into corrugated center, carefully cut around outline with craft knife. Peel off top cardboard layer from around bear, exposing corrugated center.

2. Referring to patterns, cut pieces from felt. Referring to photo throughout (page 64), glue eyes, snout, coat and shoes to bear. Glue highlights to eyes, nose/mouth to snout, and hands over coat.

3. Using black paint, add "stitching lines" around bear and clothing as shown on patterns; let dry.

4. Insert ends of wire into top corners of cardboard; twist ends closed around pencil; twist wire around pencil to shape. Tie raffia around wire in bow. ❂

—Design by Janna Britton

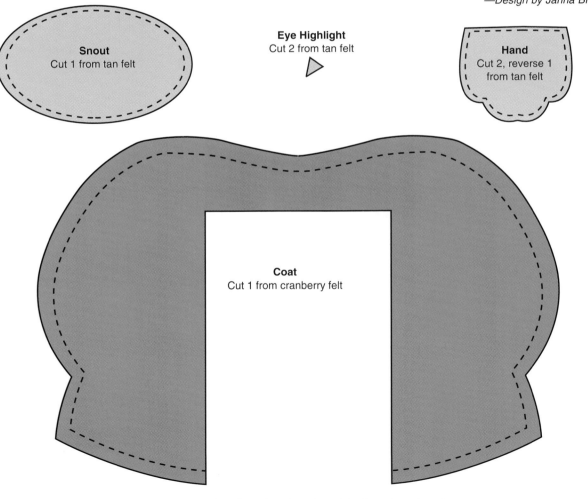

Snout
Cut 1 from tan felt

Eye Highlight
Cut 2 from tan felt

Hand
Cut 2, reverse 1
from tan felt

Coat
Cut 1 from cranberry felt

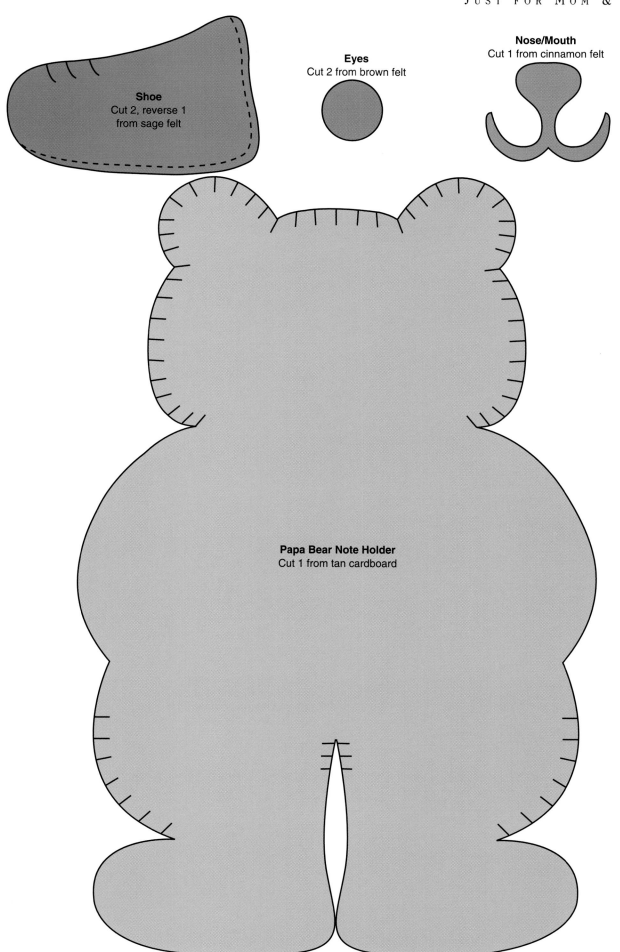

Shoe
Cut 2, reverse 1
from sage felt

Eyes
Cut 2 from brown felt

Nose/Mouth
Cut 1 from cinnamon felt

Papa Bear Note Holder
Cut 1 from tan cardboard

Cardboard Sunflower Frame

Preserve a favorite snapshot in this charming frame with a down-home touch.

Materials

- Cardboard
- Corrugated cardboard
- 3¼" circle gold print fabric or 1½"-wide gold print fabric yo-yo
- 2 (3") squares of green print fabric
- Compass
- Sewing needle
- Coordinating gold sewing thread
- Tacky craft glue
- 4 (19") strands raffia
- 12" jute twine
- ½" brown shank button
- 3½" x 5" photograph

4. Referring to photo throughout (page 65), tie raffia in wide bow. Center and glue atop opening in corrugated cardboard; let dry.

5. Glue yo-yo on top of green fabric leaves; let dry. Glue leaves and flower atop bow; let dry.

6. Glue ends of jute to back of corrugated cardboard frame front; let dry.

7. Glue corrugated cardboard onto cardboard backing, leaving ½" all around inner edge of frame and right side of frame unglued. Let dry.

8. Insert photograph. ❋

—*Design by Helen F. Rafson*

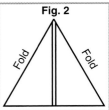

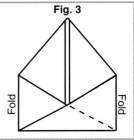

Instructions

1. Referring to pattern (see below), cut out cardboard for backing and corrugated cardboard for frame front.

2. Fold edges of gold fabric to wrong side. Sew running stitch around edges and pull thread tight to form circle. Knot; cut thread. Glue button to center of yo-yo.

3. Referring to Fig. 1, fold green fabric in half and press. Bring side

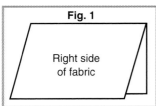

edges to center, forming right angle in center (Fig. 2); press. Bring bottom edges to center, forming right angle on each side edge (Fig. 3). Glue edges down; let dry.

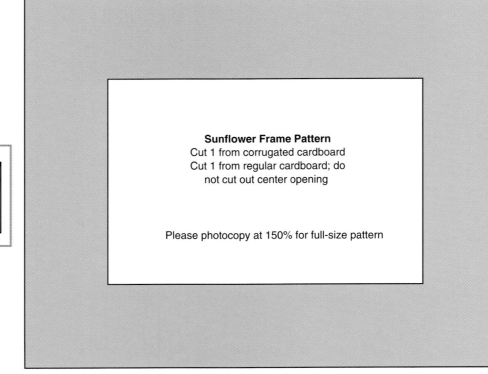

Sunflower Frame Pattern
Cut 1 from corrugated cardboard
Cut 1 from regular cardboard; do not cut out center opening

Please photocopy at 150% for full-size pattern

World's Best Mom Card

This lovely handmade card has loads of heirloom-style charm, and an added bonus—a lovely brooch!

Materials

Card

- 4" squares of heavyweight paper: ivory and tan
- 3¾" x 5½" piece dusty pink print fabric
- Coats Instant Stick & Hold for Crafts double-stick adhesive
- Deckle-edge scissors
- 4½" x 6" blank greeting card
- 2 (4") pieces of 2"-wide ivory satin ribbon

- 15 small velvet leaves, stems removed
- 20 yellow double-end pearl stamens
- Tacky craft glue

Brooch

- Jesse James & Co. buttons:
  - 3 (1") pearl flat buttons
  - 2 crystal heart buttons
  - 2 (¾") pink flat buttons
  - 2 pink rose shank buttons

- Pearl rose shank button
- Old scissors or wire cutters
- Jesse James & Co. floral trims:
  - Antique rose silk rosebud
  - Antique rose ribbon carnation
- 1½" pin back
- 2" x ½" lightweight cardboard

Card

1. Back paper squares and fabric rectangle with double-stick adhesive.

2. Referring to patterns (see below), trace hearts on back of tan and ivory papers; cut out, cutting out tan heart with deckle-edge scissors.

3. Remove backing from fabric; referring to photo throughout, fuse to card.

4. Cut V at bottom of each ribbon piece. Remove paper backing from tan heart; lay heart facedown. Fold pearl stamens unevenly (see Fig. 1) and stick them in clusters around heart. Add leaves, then ribbons.

5. Add small line of tacky craft glue around edge of tan heart behind leaves and ribbon. Fuse tan heart to card.

6. Remove backing from ivory heart; fuse atop tan

Continued on page 75

Fig. 1

Fold stamens different ways, not all in half

Cut 1 from tan on fold; trim with deckle-edge cutter

Heart Pattern
Cut 1 from ivory on fold

Fold

Bouquet of Kisses

*This sweet gift will please both the eye and the palate
with toothsome treats cleverly wrapped to resembled red rosebuds.*

Materials
- Vase
- Red shredded paper
- 12 (5½") squares red Mylar gift wrap
- 24 foil-wrapped chocolate kisses
- 12 thick, green, fabric-wrapped floral wires
- Thin, green, fabric-wrapped floral wires
- 3 red silk roses on stems
- 4 stems artificial white baby's breath
- Stems of silk rose leaves
- 3 yards 2½"-wide plaid wire-edge ribbon
- Wire cutters
- Cellophane tape
- Hot-glue gun

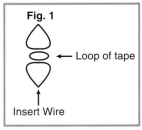

Instructions

1. Pack vase firmly with red shredded paper.

2. Referring to Fig. 1, tape two candy kisses together, end to end. Insert a thick floral wire into the tip of one of the kisses.

3. Place candy on Mylar square. Cover candy by folding Mylar as shown in Fig. 2.

Fig. 1

← Loop of tape

↑ Insert Wire

4. Wrap thin floral wire around Mylar at base of candy kisses. Twist to secure; trim wire ends with wire cutters. Trim Mylar evenly around base of chocolate rosebud.

5. Position rose leaves on stem; secure with a dot of glue, if necessary.

6. Repeat with remaining kisses to make a dozen candy rosebuds.

7. Insert baby's breath, silk roses and candy rosebuds in vase in a pleasing arrangement, trimming stems with wire cutters as needed.

Continued on page 75

Fig. 2

←Twist

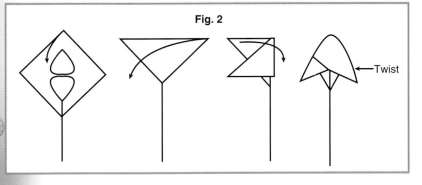

Pillar Candle

Candles such as this are all the rage in gift shops, but can they be pricey!
Create your own—with the colors and flowers you prefer—
by adding a few dried petals to an inexpensive purchased candle.

Materials
- 6" ivory 2¾"-diameter pillar candle
- 2 pressed tansy leaves
- 3 pressed sprigs of Jacob's ladder
- 2 pressed pink azalea blossoms
- Pressed blue viola
- Pressed yellow viola
- 3 pressed phlox stems
- Plaid's Modge Podge decoupage medium in matté finish
- #3 round artist's brush
- ½" wash artist's brush
- Flat-tip tweezers for pressed flowers

Project Notes

If listed varieties of flowers aren't available as purchased pressed flowers, you can press your own, using a variety from your garden or fresh flowers purchased from a florist.

Place flowers to dry between two sheets of white paper, then place paper between pages of a phone book for two or three weeks, until blossoms are completely dry. If pressing your own, experiment with a variety to see which ones dry well for you.

Always press more than you think you'll need to allow for damage.

Decoupage-medium-coated candle is safe to burn, but take care if flame is allowed to reach flowers, as they can cause wax to drip or flare slightly. Never leave a burning candle unattended, and always burn on a heat-proof surface.

Instructions

1. Referring to photo throughout, use wash brush to paint area to be decorated with decoupage medium.

2. Handling flowers with tweezers to avoid damage, position background leaves, flowers and sprigs as shown, laying each in wet decoupage medium, then applying more medium with round brush to seal flowers in place. Work from back layer to front, coating each layer lightly so next layer will adhere.

3. When all flowers are positioned as desired, allow candle to dry completely.

4. Using wash brush, apply overcoat of decoupage medium to all sides of candle, taking care to avoid obvious brush strokes. It is not necessary to coat top of candle. Let dry completely before handling. ✿

—Design by Creative Chi

Mother-Daughter Aprons

Mother and daughter sharing hours in the kitchen is a time-honored tradition. It will be even more fun in these special aprons!

Materials

- ¼ yard red-hearts-on-white print fabric
- Adult-size red apron #0150 from BagWorks, Inc.
- Child-size red apron #0146 from BagWorks, Inc.
- Slick white Tulip dimensional paint
- Washable fabric glue
- Heavy cardboard
- Cotton swab
- Large plastic bag

Instructions

1. Prewash aprons without fabric softener; dry thoroughly.

2. Referring to patterns (see below and page 74), trace letters onto heavy cardboard; cut out. Use cardboard patterns to trace letters onto fabric (if you trace letters onto wrong side of fabric, be sure to reverse letters).

3. Referring to photo throughout, lay out "I LOVE COOKING" and five hearts on adult apron. Lay out "I DO TOO" and three hearts on child's apron.

4. Working with one letter/heart at a time, attach to apron: Place right side of fabric facedown on paper plate. Apply thin coat of glue to back with cotton swab. Carefully replace letter on apron, glue side down. Allow to dry completely.

5. When glue is dry, iron apron on wrong side to heat-set glue and remove any folds. Or, place aprons in dryer at high heat for five to 10 minutes.

6. Place aprons right side up on large plastic bag on large flat surface. Outline each letter and heart with white dimensional paint; let dry completely, for four to six hours. ❀

—Designs by Mary T. Cosgrove

Letter Graphs

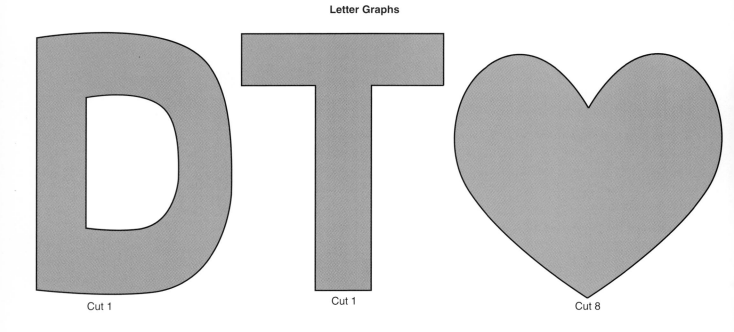

Cut 1

Cut 1

Cut 8

Letter Graphs

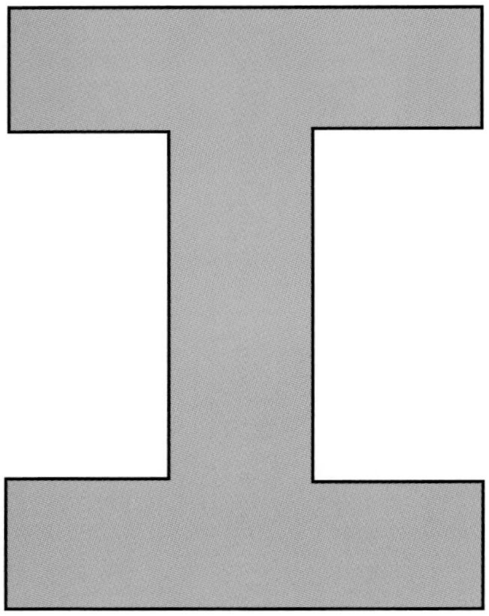

I
Cut 3

L
Cut 1

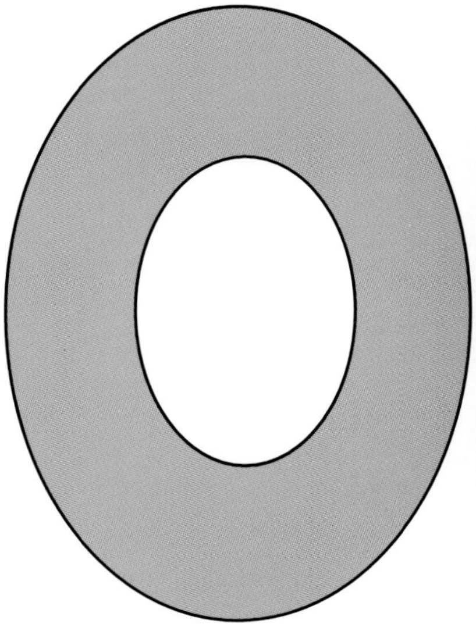

O
Cut 6

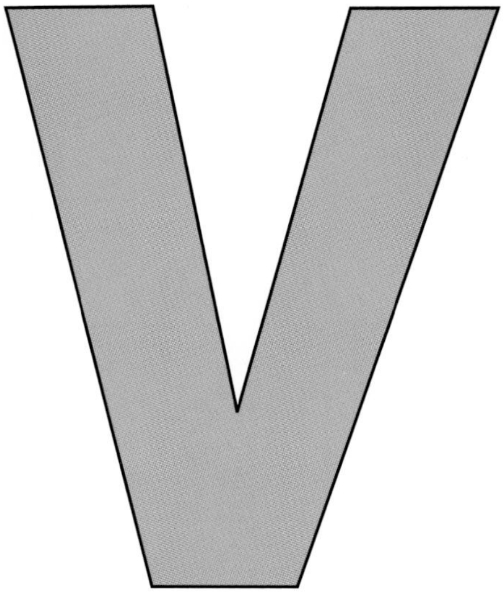

V
Cut 1

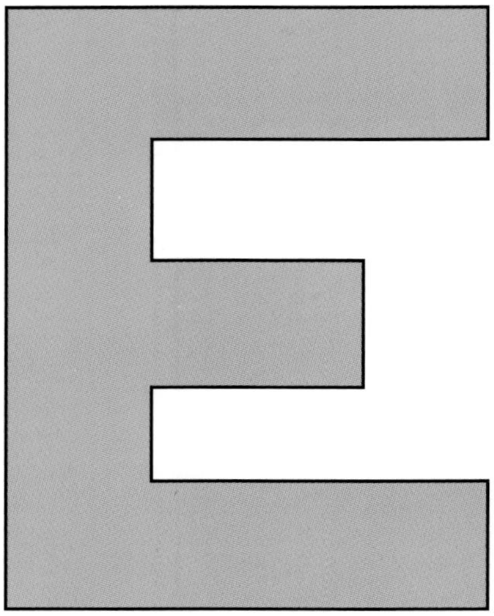

E
Cut 1

C
Cut 1

K
Cut 1

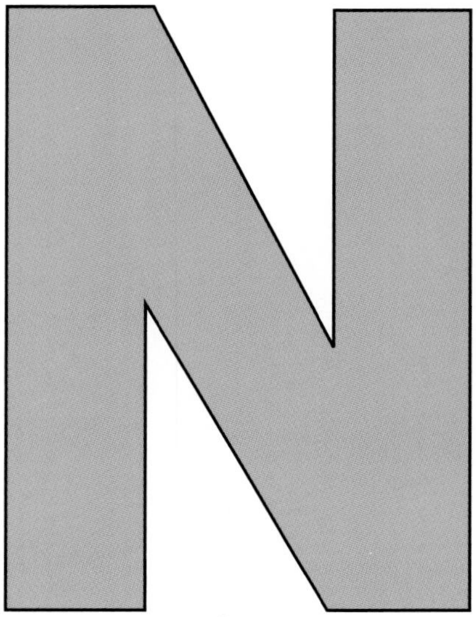

N
Cut 1

G
Cut 1

Twig Bundle

Share the colors of spring with this lovely cluster of artfully arranged twigs and dried flowers. Even if you've never fancied yourself a floral designer, you'll love the results!

Materials

- 8–10 (8") knobby twigs (see Project Note)
- 2 stalks dried pink larkspur
- 2 stalks dried blue larkspur
- 7 yellow strawflowers
- Small pink strawflower
- Large burgundy strawflower
- 10 dried pink rosebuds
- 6 sprigs dried German statice
- Dried green Springerii fern
- Green paddle wire
- Low-temperature glue gun

Project Note

Sample was completed using dogwood twigs.

Instructions

1. Gather twigs into bundle for base; wrap with paddle wire to secure. Twist wire ends to make hanging loop on center back.

2. Referring to photo throughout, glue fern and larkspur onto twigs for background. Add statice to both sides.

3. Glue burgundy strawflower to center front; glue pink strawflower just below it. Add yellow strawflowers around sides and over top.

4. Fill in gaps in design with rosebuds. ✿

—*Design by Creative Chi*

World's Best Mom Card

Continued from page 69

heart. If you wish, card is complete at this point. Write a message on the heart or leave it plain.

Brooch

1. If adding brooch to card, pierce holes through heart so pin can be displayed on card.

2. Glue ¾" pink flat buttons to ends of lightweight cardboard, extending buttons beyond edges so brooch measures 2" long.

3. Glue two 1" pearl buttons to base of brooch so that they overlap pink buttons; glue third pearl flat button in center, overlapping previous pearl buttons. Let brooch dry completely.

4. Using old scissors or wire cutters, cut shanks from rose buttons. (Wear eye protection in case shanks fly off, and dispose of shanks carefully.) Glue rose buttons, crystal hearts and silk and ribbon flowers to brooch. Let dry.

5. Glue pin back to back of brooch. ✿

—*Design by Judi Kauffman*

Bouquet of Kisses

Continued from page 70

8. Wrap ribbon around vase; overlap ends 1" and cut off excess. Glue ends to secure.

9. From remaining ribbon, make a bow with three loops on each side; secure at center with narrow wrapped floral wire. Wire or glue bow over overlapped ribbon ends. ✿

—*Design by Beth Wheeler*

Flowerpot Trio

Surprise your mom on her special day with this little pot of cheerful blossoms that will never droop or fade! You can't overwater them—and in fact, they thrive in extreme heat!

Materials

- 1" x 1⅛" flowerpot
- Acrylic craft paint: cream and hunter green
- Paintbrush
- 3 round wooden toothpicks
- Sculpey III modeling compound by Polyform:
  Green #022
  Yellow #072
  Dusty rose #303
  Peach #392
  Turquoise #505
- Craft knife with straight blade
- 6 black seed beads
- Straight pin
- Craft glue
- Polyester fiberfill
- Spanish moss
- Hot-glue gun

Project Note

Refer to photo throughout.

Instructions

1. Paint flowerpot with cream paint; let dry completely.

2. Cut toothpicks into different lengths for stems; paint hunter green. Set aside to dry; paint with a second coat, if needed.

3. Cut a quarter-section from dusty rose modeling compound. Cut this section in half, and cut one of these halves in half again. Do this once more so that you have ⅛ of the original quarter-section.

4. Soften compound with your fingers; roll into a ball between your palms and flatten into disk about ¾" wide and ¼" thick.

5. With cutting edge, cut petals of equal width from outside about halfway to center. Carefully indent center of flower with tip of your little finger. Push pointed end of one painted toothpick into flower between two petals for stem.

6. Flatten a pea-size ball of yellow modeling compound; press gently into indented flower center.

7. Referring to Fig. 1, add face, checking to make sure stem is at bottom of flower: Press a pair of seed beads on their sides into face for eyes, pressing them into compound until holes can no longer be seen. Roll a tiny ball of yellow compound for nose. Add additional facial features—eyelashes, eyebrows, mouth—with straight pin.

Fig. 1

8. Following the same procedure, make another flower from turquoise modeling compound.

9. Repeat step 3 using peach modeling compound. Cut resulting piece in half again to make a smaller flower. Flatten into a ⅝"-wide disk ⅛" thick. Make petals, indent center and insert toothpick stem, as for other flowers.

10. Roll a piece of yellow modeling compound somewhat smaller than a pea for smaller flower's face. Flatten and press gently in place. Add seed bead eyes. Add nose with tiny ball of yellow. Add facial features with straight pin.

11. Soften two pea-size balls of green modeling compound. Roll and flatten into two teardrop shapes for leaves. Using straight edge, press center vein in each leaf.

Continued on page 80

Mom's Memory Album

Create a personalized memory album featuring the artwork of your favorite pint-size artist; or, use our patterns for a whimsical treatment.

Materials

- Kid's artwork or patterns provided
- 10" x 14" muslin
- Air-soluble marking pen
- Duncan Scribbles fabric paints: red, yellow, blue and green
- Paintbrushes
- Checkerboard stencil or foam stamp
- Black fine-point permanent marker
- 8½" x 11" stiff cardboard
- Quilt batting
- Hot-glue gun
- Jumbo red piping
- Scrapbook album

Instructions

1. Make a photocopy of your child's artwork (or duplicate our pattern pieces, page 78). Cut out main components to use as patterns.

2. Referring to photo throughout, position patterns on muslin; trace with air-soluble pen.

3. Paint shapes. (If using our design, use checkerboard pattern or square cut from sponge to stamp checkerboard pattern across bottom of muslin.) Let dry completely. Heat-set as instructed by paint manufacturer.

4. Using marking pen, outline shapes and add "stitches" and other details.

5. Round off corners of cardboard with scissors. Using cardboard as a pattern, cut two pieces of quilt batting to match; glue both to same side of cardboard.

6. Center cardboard batting side down on wrong side of

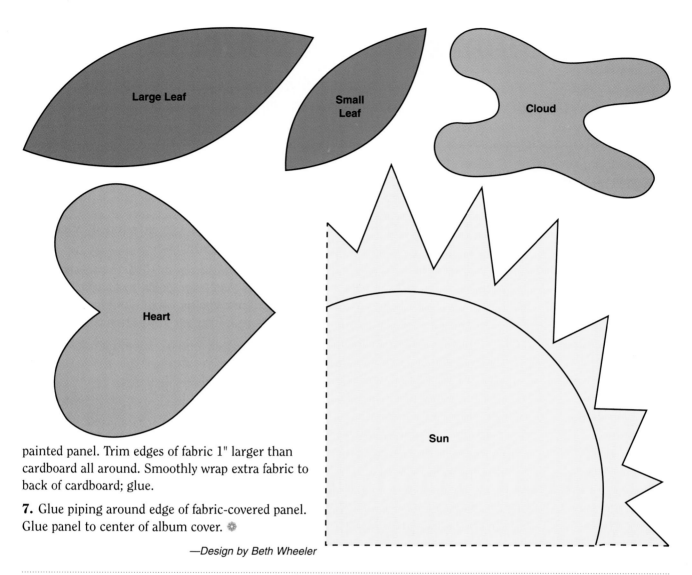

Large Leaf

Small Leaf

Cloud

Heart

Sun

painted panel. Trim edges of fabric 1" larger than cardboard all around. Smoothly wrap extra fabric to back of cardboard; glue.

7. Glue piping around edge of fabric-covered panel. Glue panel to center of album cover. ✱

—Design by Beth Wheeler

Bouquet of Roses Vest

Surprise Mom with a pretty vest adorned with simple roses and twining leaves. It takes less than an hour to complete!

Materials
- Muslin or canvas vest
- T-shirt board
- Straight pins or masking tape
- 4 (3" x 4½") compressed sponges
- 3 rubber bands
- Duncan Scribbles fabric paints: white, pink and wine
- Duncan Scribbles Dimensional fabric paints: green and plum
- Paper plate
- Paintbrushes
- Craft stick

Instructions

1. Secure vest on T-shirt board with pins or masking tape.

2. Tightly roll one sponge while still flat; fasten with

rubber band close to one end. Expand in clean water; squeeze out excess moisture. (See Fig. 1, page 80.)

3. Expand remaining sponges in clean water. Squeeze

out excess moisture. Roll one sponge as tightly as possible; secure with a rubber band wrapped near one end.

4. Roll another sponge as tightly as possible. Roll remaining sponge around it (Fig. 2); secure with a rubber band close to one end.

5. Squeeze small puddle of white paint onto paper plate. Squeeze small puddles of pink and wine close to white. Swirl three colors together with craft stick.

6. Dab large sponge into puddle; dab on paper plate to remove excess. Referring to photo throughout, press paint-filled sponge to vest to make large roses. Repeat with medium and small sponges, squeezing and swirling more paint onto paper plate as needed.

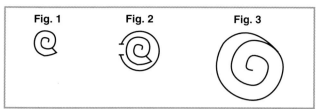

Fig. 1   Fig. 2   Fig. 3

7. Allow painted vest to dry; heat-set as directed by manufacturer.

8. Define each rose by squeezing plum dimensional paint over blossom in a spiral pattern (Fig. 3). Let dry.

9. Add vines and leaves with green dimensional paint. Let dry completely before wearing. ❀

—*Design by Beth Wheeler*

Flowerpot Trio

Continued from page 76

12. Preheat oven to 275 degrees. Remove toothpick stems from flowers; carefully place flowers and leaves on ovenproof plate. Bake for 10 minutes; let cool completely.

13. Squeeze craft glue into flowerpot; place a small amount of stuffing inside (stuffing should not show above top of pot). Using hot-glue gun, glue a small amount of

Spanish moss on top of stuffing; trim as needed.

14. Apply glue from hot-glue gun to blunt ends of stems; push into Spanish moss and stuffing, placing shortest toothpick in front of the other two. Using craft glue, glue cooled flowers onto toothpicks; glue leaves onto Spanish moss, one beside each of the taller flowers in back. ❀

—*Design by Jackie Haskell*

"I Love You" Pin

How long will you slave to make this lovely, heirloom-style brooch for your mom or another special person? Ten whole minutes!

Materials
- Tacky craft glue
- 2½" x 1⅝" Simply Stitches silk ribbon embroidery appliqué
- 2¾" x 2½" Battenberg lace heart from Wimpole Street Creations
- Sewing needle and white thread
- 7 (4mm) white pearl beads
- Hot-glue gun
- Brass "I love you" charm from Creative Beginnings
- Pin back

Instructions

1. Apply a thin layer of tacky craft glue over entire back of embroidered appliqué except the two uppermost buds, which will overlap brass charm. Referring to photo throughout, press appliqué onto front of lace heart.

Continued on page 84

Gift Bag

Those beautiful gift bags are lovely, but pricey! Here's a versatile design that will let you create your own, matching each perfectly to the gift, the season and the lucky recipient.

Materials
- Gift bag with handles
- Plain paper
- Small pieces of 2 coordinating fabrics
- Fusible sheet
- Thin cardboard
- Acrylic paints: tan and white
- Dimensional paints: deep pink, green and white
- Paintbrush
- 4 coordinating colors of 6-strand embroidery floss
- 5 (⅞") wooden hearts
- Pinking shears or wave blade
- Low-temperature glue gun
- Toothpick

Instructions

1. Cut fabric for front of bag: Bond fusible sheet to wrong side of fabric. Cut fabric with pinking shears. (On our sample, fabric is approximately 8½" square.) Position fabric on front of bag; fuse in place.

2. Bond fusible sheet to wrong side of plain paper. With pinking shears, cut paper smaller than fabric (on our sample, it measures approximately 6½" W x 5¼" H).

3. Remove paper backing; fuse paper to fabric panel.

4. Referring to photo throughout, cut four simple spool shapes (approximately 1" W x 1¼" H) from thin cardboard. Paint spools tan; let dry. Paint wooden hearts with white acrylic; let dry.

5. Onto each painted heart, squeeze one drop deep pink and one drop white dimensional paint, side by side. Gently swirl clockwise through both paint drops with toothpick, swirling paints together to make rosebud. Squeeze a small green dot on each side of rosebud; using toothpick, extend green drops into leaf shapes. Let dry completely.

6. Wrap a different color of embroidery floss around each spool, anchoring floss ends on back.

7. Referring to photo throughout, glue a heart over floss in the center of each spool. Glue spools around edge of paper.

8. Fuse two long strips of coordinating fabrics together, wrong sides facing. Trim with pinking shears. Tie in a bow around one bag handle.

9. Referring to photo, add name to bag using deep pink dimensional paint. Glue remaining heart below name.

—Design by Beth Wheeler

Tulip Pencil Can & Pencil Toppers

This pretty set of desktop helpers makes a thoughtful gift for Mom—
and it's simple enough that even the youngsters can help.

Materials
Pencil Can
- Soup can with 1 end cut out
- Sandpaper or plastic tape or masking tape
- Jute twine
- Expandable sponge
- Acrylic paints: orange, red, fuchsia and green
- Cotton swabs
- Tacky craft glue

Pencil Toppers
- Black permanent fine-tip marker
- Craft foam sheets—green, red and fuchsia
- Orange pipe cleaner
- Tacky craft glue
- 2 yellow No. 2 pencils

Instructions

Pencil Can

1. Wash can thoroughly; dry. Sand any sharp or rough edges, or cover with plastic or masking tape.

2. Apply glue to outside of can. Beginning at top, wrap can with jute, pushing strands together so can is covered tightly and smoothly. Let dry completely.

3. Trace patterns. Cut two squares, one tulip and one set of leaves from dry sponge. Immerse sponge in water; wring out.

4. Dip side of one square sponge in fuchsia paint and the other in orange. Referring to photo, stamp alternating border of squares around top and bottom of can. Let dry.

5. Using cotton swab, paint red dots in center of each orange square. Let dry.

6. Dip tulip in red paint; stamp three tulips spaced evenly around middle of can. Let dry.

7. Dip leaves in green paint; stamp three sets of stems and leaves below tulips around middle of can. Let dry.

Continued on page 88

Leaves
Cut 1 from sponge
and 2 from green
craft foam

Tulip
Cut 1 from sponge,
1 from red craft foam, and
1 from fuchsia craft foam

Square Sponge Pattern
Cut 2 from sponge

Southwestern-Style
Pencil Can & Pencil Toppers

*With minimal help from you, the youngsters can have a lot of fun
creating this special gift in plenty of time for Father's Day.*

Materials

Pencil Can

- Soup can with 1 end cut out
- Sandpaper or plastic tape or masking tape
- Jute twine
- Expandable sponge

- Acrylic paints: brown, dark green and metallic gold

Pencil Toppers

- Black permanent fine-tip marker
- Craft foam sheets: brown and green
- Acrylic paint: metallic gold

- Brown pipe cleaner
- 2 dark green No. 2 pencils

Both Projects

- Cotton swabs
- Tacky craft glue

Instructions

Pencil Can

1. Wash can thoroughly; dry. Sand any sharp or rough edges, or cover with plastic or masking tape.

2. Apply glue to outside of can. Beginning at top, wrap can with jute, pushing strands together so can is covered tightly and smoothly. Let dry completely.

3. Referring to patterns, cut two

Continued on page 88

Larger Diamond
Cut 1 from sponge
and 2 from green craft foam

Square Sponge Pattern
Cut 2 from sponge

Smaller Diamond
Cut 1 from sponge and
2 from brown craft foam

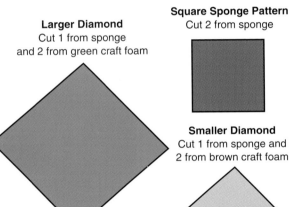

Father-Son Visors

*It's hard to know who will be prouder to wear these special visors—
the adoring dad or the equally adoring son! They stitch up in a hurry!*

Materials

- Crafter's Pride adult-size visor with 14-count Aida panel from Daniel Enterprises
- Crafter's Pride child-size visor with 14-count Aida panel from Daniel Enterprises
- Madeira's Decora rayon embroidery floss as listed in color key
- Dazzlers Liquid Stars patriotic medley Soft Fabric Paint by Delta Technical Coatings
- Small paintbrush

Instructions

1. Count threads in stitching areas on both visors to find centers; mark with straight pin or basting thread, if desired. Match center of visor to center of stitching on graph and Cross Stitch as shown, using 2 strands rayon embroidery floss. Backstitch hyphens in matching colors.

2. Using small paintbrush, paint the 14-count Aida fabric around the stitching with glitter-and-stars fabric paint; set aside to dry completely. ❀

—*Designs by Mary T. Cosgrove*

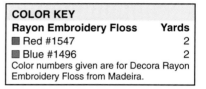

COLOR KEY	
Rayon Embroidery Floss	**Yards**
■ Red #1547	2
■ Blue #1496	2
Color numbers given are for Decora Rayon Embroidery Floss from Madeira.	

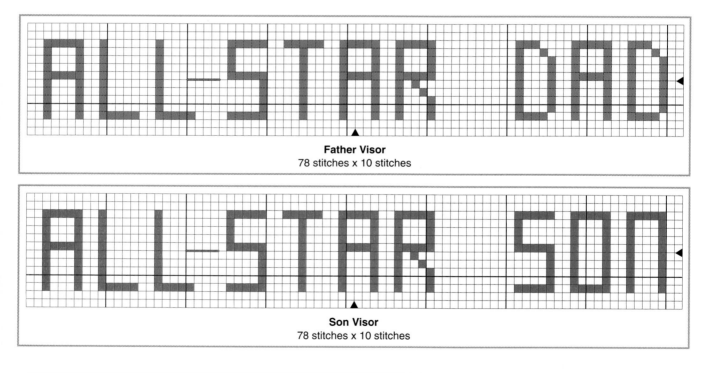

Father Visor
78 stitches x 10 stitches

Son Visor
78 stitches x 10 stitches

I Love You Pin

Continued from page 80

2. Using doubled thread, sew pearl beads onto pin.

3. Using glue gun, glue brass charm to top of pin. Apply a tiny amount of hot glue to backs of uppermost buds; press in place over front of brass charm.

4. Sew pin back to back of heart. ❀

—*Design by Christine Malone*

Dad's Mini Fish Banners

Here's a catch Dad will love! These cute quilted banners will look great hanging in the den—and they'll never jump the hook!

Materials

Green Banner

- Fabric scraps: 4 green print fabrics and natural muslin
- 5" x 7" piece green checked fabric
- 3½" x 5½" low-loft batting
- ½" green flat button
- 2 size 1 brass safety snap swivels (found in fishing supplies)
- 20" jute twine
- 10"–12" piece curved tree branch
- Paper
- Matching sewing threads
- Tweezers

Pattern Notes

These mini quilts are pieced together with the quick and easy technique of "foundation piecing." This very accurate piecing process eliminates the need for templates and cutting out each fabric piece precisely.

For each pattern, trace all lines and numbers onto a piece of plain paper. Numbers indicate the order in which each piece is sewn.

Cut out the body and tail patterns on the solid outer line only. Fabric pieces do not have to be cut precisely, but should be large enough to completely cover the numbered area and extend at least ½" beyond seam line on all sides.

The fabric is held on the bottom (unprinted) side of paper; sewing is done on printed side of paper, directly on the lines through paper and fabric. When all seams are completed, paper is torn away.

Set sewing machine stitch length to 12–15 stitches per inch so stitching is very secure and paper tears away more easily.

Instructions

Green Banner

1. Place tracing paper over Fin 1 pattern. Trace; cut out. Place pattern over doubled piece of print fabric, right sides facing, and trace around pattern. Sew on traced lines, leaving an opening for turning. Cut ⅛" from stitched line; clip corners. Turn right side out and press.

2. Center a piece of print fabric right side up over Section 1 on the back (unmarked) side of paper. Hold paper up to light to make sure edges of fabric extend at least ½" beyond seam line on all sides. Hold this first piece in place with a pin.

Continued on page 88

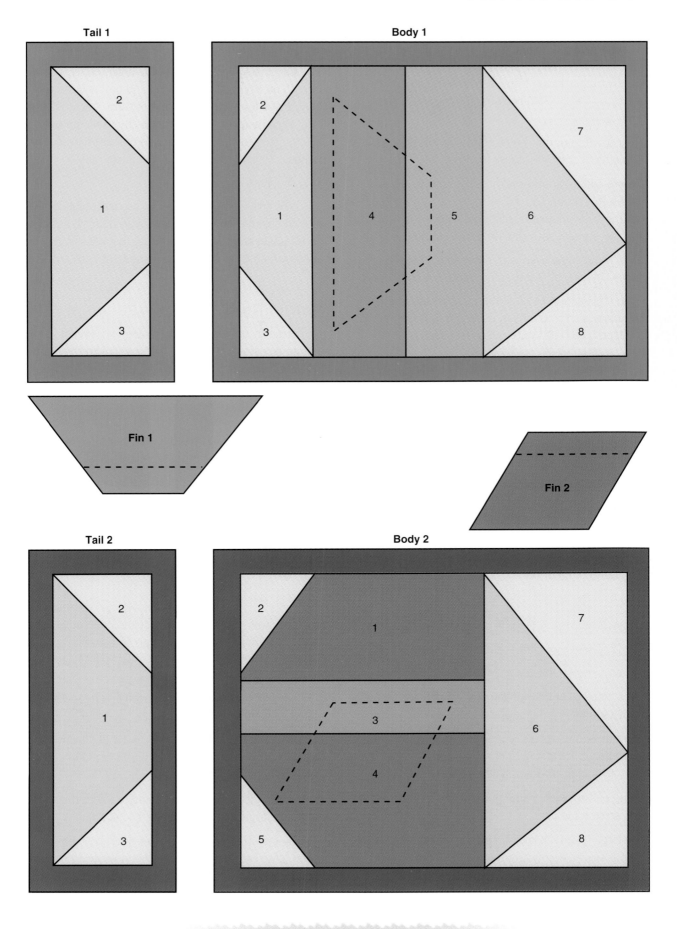

Tail 1

Body 1

Fin 1

Fin 2

Tail 2

Body 2

3. Place muslin for Section 2 on first print piece, right sides facing, and pin. Turn paper over and sew on line between 1 and 2, extending the stitching two or three stitches beyond line at beginning and end. Trim seam ⅛"–¼". Fold back muslin piece (2), right side up, and press.

4. Repeat with another piece of muslin for Section 3. Add middle Section 4 in same manner.

5. Before adding another print to Section 5, pin prepared fin to Section 4 so ¼" of raw edge of fin will be in seam line. Sew on Sections 5 and 6 with remaining prints and 7 and 8 with muslin. Press carefully.

6. Trim outer edges even with outer edge of paper, which includes ¼" seam allowance all around. Set body aside.

7. Make tail section in same manner, using same fabric as head for Tail 1 and muslin for 2 and 3. Press and trim outer edges even with outer edges of paper.

8. To join tail and body sections, place right sides together and match seam lines with help of pins. Sew on line. Press seam open.

9. Carefully remove paper backing one section at a time, using tweezers if necessary. Press completed block.

10. Lay checked fabric right side down on work surface. Center batting on backing and pin or baste to hold. Press long edges (top and bottom) down ¼". Fold long ends in again to cover seam allowance on fish block; press and pin. Hand-stitch top and bottom border in place. Repeat with borders on short ends.

11. Sew button on for eye.

12. Sew swivel end of hanger to top back of completed block 1" from each end. Cut twine in half; tie top of each hanger to branch by running twine through eyelet and around branch. Tie in bow and trim ends.

Blue Banner

Substitute blue fabrics for greens.

Construct in same manner as green fish, except use Fin 2 and place fin over Section 4 and sew it in the seam between Sections 3 and 4. ❁

—Designs by Chris Malone

Tulip Pencil Can & Pencil Toppers

Continued from page 82

8. Using swab, paint orange dots between tulips. Let dry.

Pencil Toppers

1. Trace patterns (see page 82) onto red, fuchsia and green craft foam; cut out.

2. With fine-tip marker, draw wavy border around insides of leaves and tulips.

3. Cut pipe cleaners to 7"; referring to photo throughout, wrap each around pencil, leaving 1" end straight at top.

4. Glue tulip to top of each leaf set; glue stem to straight end of pipe cleaner. Let dry. ❁

—Designs by Helen L. Rafson

Southwestern-Style Pencil Can & Pencil Toppers

Continued from page 83

squares, one larger diamond and one smaller diamond from dry sponge. Immerse sponge in water; wring out.

4. Dip side of one square sponge in brown paint and the other in green. Referring to photo, stamp alternating border of squares around top and bottom of can. Let dry.

5. Using cotton swab, paint gold dots in center of each brown square. Let dry.

6. Dip larger diamond sponge in green paint; stamp three diamonds spaced evenly around middle of can. Let dry.

7. Sponge smaller brown diamond over each green diamond; let dry.

8. Using swab, paint gold dots in centers of brown diamond and brown spots between green diamonds. Let dry.

Pencil Toppers

1. Trace patterns (see page 83) onto brown and green craft foam; cut out.

2. With fine-tip marker, draw wavy border around diamonds. Using cotton swab, paint gold circle in center of each brown diamond; let dry.

3. Cut pipe cleaners to 7"; referring to photo throughout, wrap each around pencil, leaving 1" end straight at top.

4. Glue brown diamond in center of each green diamond; glue each assembled diamond to straight end of pipe cleaner. Let dry. ❁

—Designs by Helen L. Rafson

"Just Like Dad" Father's Day Card

This card would be fun to make with a group of children. Inexpensive pompons and wiggle eyes make this project a perfect choice for a class or Scout troop.

Materials

- Blank greeting card with deckle edge
- Fine-point markers
- 20 (⅜") pompons in color of your choice
- 6 (4mm) movable eyes
- 2 (6mm) movable eyes
- Coats Instant Stick & Hold double-stick adhesive
- Tacky craft glue

Instructions

1. Cut a long, ⅛"-wide strip from double-stick adhesive that looks like a worm; cut a 3" piece and a 4" piece.

2. Remove paper backing. Referring to photo throughout, fuse to front of card where the two caterpillars will crawl, the smaller caterpillar on top. Remove paper backing.

3. Stick seven pompons to top strip and 11 to bottom strip.

4. Using markers, draw antennae and legs and write message: "Dad, I want to be just like you when I grow up!" Decorate with squiggles and dots.

5. Glue two smaller eyes to smaller caterpillar and larger eyes to larger caterpillar.

6. Decorate the envelope with extra pompon faces, including eyes and antennae. ✿

—Design by Judi Kauffman

An American Celebration

Celebrate the freedoms and blessings of living in America with this collection of patriotic crafts! You'll find projects for decorating this year's Fourth of July family reunion and crafts for adding a charming Americana feel to your home year-round.

Patriotic Angel

It takes less than two hours to create this cheerful holiday angel in red, white and blue!

Materials

- Bendi Doll from Wimpole Street Creations
- 1 yard 6"-wide ecru satin ribbon with wire at one edge and 1"–2" from other edge (see Fig. 1)
- 1⅓ yards 2½"-wide red-and-white striped fabric ribbon with wire at both edges
- 2⅓ yards ⅛"-wide red satin ribbon
- 1¼ yards ³⁄₁₆"-wide red picot-edge ribbon
- Wired star garlands: red, white and blue
- Star spangles: red and blue
- Black fine-tip permanent marking pen
- Colored pencils: pink and orange
- Black seed beads
- Sewing needle and off-white thread
- Blond curly doll hair
- Fabric glue
- Hot-glue gun

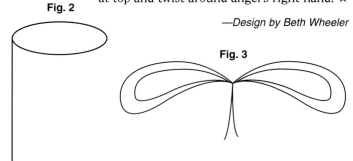

Instructions

1. Referring to photo throughout (page 90), give angel a dress by wrapping ecru wired ribbon around doll just under arms; wired edge should be at hem and seam should be in back. Gently pull top wire (1"–2" from edge) to gather ribbon to fit as a bodice. Twist wire ends in back to secure; clip off excess. Turn raw fabric edges under; glue.

2. Cut two 10" pieces striped ribbon for sleeves; pull wires along both edges to gather one piece around arm; clip excess wire. Repeat with other piece on other arm. Secure sleeves at shoulders with a dot of fabric glue.

3. For apron, wrap remaining striped ribbon around angel's waist over wide satin ribbon; pull wire in upper edge to gather; twist ends to secure at center back and clip excess.

4. Using glue gun, glue red spangles along hem of satin dress; glue blue spangles along hem of apron. Glue a single red spangle to center of bodice.

5. Using fabric glue, tack upper edge of bodice to angel's body behind spangle to hold it in place.

6. Crisscross ⅛"-wide ribbon around angel's legs; secure with dots of glue. Cut picot-edge ribbon in three

equal pieces; tie one piece in a bow; repeat with another piece. Tie third piece in a bow around angel's wrist. Trim ends to about 4"; cut ends at an angle and glue blue spangle to end of each streamer. Glue bow over top of each foot; glue blue spangle over center of bow.

7. With marking pen, draw deep "U" on angel's face for smile. Color cheeks with pink colored pencil and nose with orange colored pencil. Sew seed beads in place for eyes, pulling thread ends from back of doll's head to indent eyes slightly.

8. Glue curly hair to doll's head.

9. Cut 15" piece of star garland. Referring to Fig. 2, twist into halo. Glue at back of head.

10. Cut 45" piece of each of the three garlands. Holding all three pieces together, coil garlands around pencil. Wrap one end of coil around angel's left hand and one around her right foot to make hanger.

11. Bend remaining blue garland into a wide bow with two loops on each side (Fig. 3); twist to secure. Glue in place between shoulders for wings.

12. Bend a small piece of garland into a wand with star at top and twist around angel's right hand. ★

—Design by Beth Wheeler

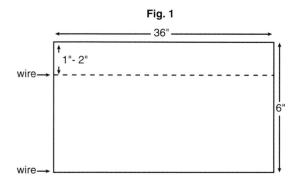

Fig. 1

Fig. 2

Fig. 3

Pig With Watermelon

All he needs is a slice of cold, juicy watermelon and this little oinker is as happy as … well, as a "hawg in a waller"! This cute critter will sit happily on the edge of your whatnot shelf, or anywhere a touch of summer fun is welcome!

Materials
- Sculpey III modeling compound by Polyform:
  - Green #022
  - Black #042
  - Red #082
  - Flesh #092
  - Ivory #501
- 2 black seed beads
- Straight-edge tool for cutting and making lines
- Straight pin with ball head

Instructions

1. Cut off a quarter-section of red modeling compound; cut this small piece in half, then cut one of the halves in half again, giving you ¼ of the original quarter-section. Soften compound between your fingers and roll into a ball. Flatten ball and shape it into a ¼"-thick half-circle, about 1" wide at its widest point.

2. Soften and work a marble-size ball of ivory modeling compound. Form into a rope by rolling it back and forth on clean tabletop with your finger. Flatten the rope to make a band as wide as the red portion is thick—about ¼". Referring to photo throughout, gently press white band around curve of red half-circle to make white of watermelon. Trim off any excess and gently shape ends.

3. Using green, repeat step 2, pressing green compound against ivory.

4. Cut off a quarter-section of flesh modeling compound; cut this piece in half, and one of the halves in half, and one of those halves in half again, leaving you with ⅛ of the original quarter-section. Soften, roll and flatten compound into a disk about ¼" thick and ⅝" wide for head.

5. Referring to Fig. 1, press black seed beads on their sides into head for eyes; press just until none of the bead hole shows. Using straight edge, indent two eyelashes for each eye.

Fig. 1

6. Form another small ball of flesh compound into a flattened oval for snout. Attach to head below eyes; with ball head of straight pin, make shallow indentations for nostrils. Place head at center top edge of watermelon.

7. For top legs, roll two pea-size balls of flesh compound into identical ropes, each with one end thicker than the other. Flatten and round thicker ends; cut an indentation in each for hoof. Position front leg on each side of head, protruding over to front of watermelon. Press excess to back and trim off extra compound.

8. For bottom legs, flatten two pea-size balls of flesh compound into identical disks about ⅜" wide. With straight edge, cut an indentation in each for hoof. Position legs at bottom of watermelon so that legs will help support figure when it is set upright.

9. For ears, cut one pea-size ball of flesh compound in half. Roll each half into a ball and flatten into teardrop shape with pointed end. Attach rounded end to top of head; fold point over to front.

10. For watermelon seeds, roll three identical, very small balls of black compound. Flatten into identical teardrop shapes; gently press to red part of watermelon.

11. Transfer molded figure to an oven-proof plate. Bake in a preheated 275-degree oven for 10 minutes; cool completely. ★

—Design by Jackie Haskell

Checkered Star

Fabric scraps and corrugated cardboard make a pretty patriotic accent to hang anywhere!

Materials

- 9" square corrugated cardboard
- Craft knife
- DecoArt Americana acrylic paint: whitewash and Santa red
- ½" flat paintbrush
- 5" square Peel n Stick double-sided adhesive by Therm O Web
- Blue-and-white plaid or checked fabric:
  5" square
  30" x 1½" strip
- 2 (½") wooden heart beads with holes through sides
- ¾" wooden heart bead with holes through sides
- 36" 20-gauge black wire
- 3 yards natural raffia

Instructions

1. Trace and cut out star pattern onto cardboard so that corrugation channels run from side to side (check edge of cardboard).

2. Using craft knife, cut through top layer of cardboard along dashed line. Peel top layer of cardboard from larger portion of star only. Clean off any extra shreds of paper from corrugated channels.

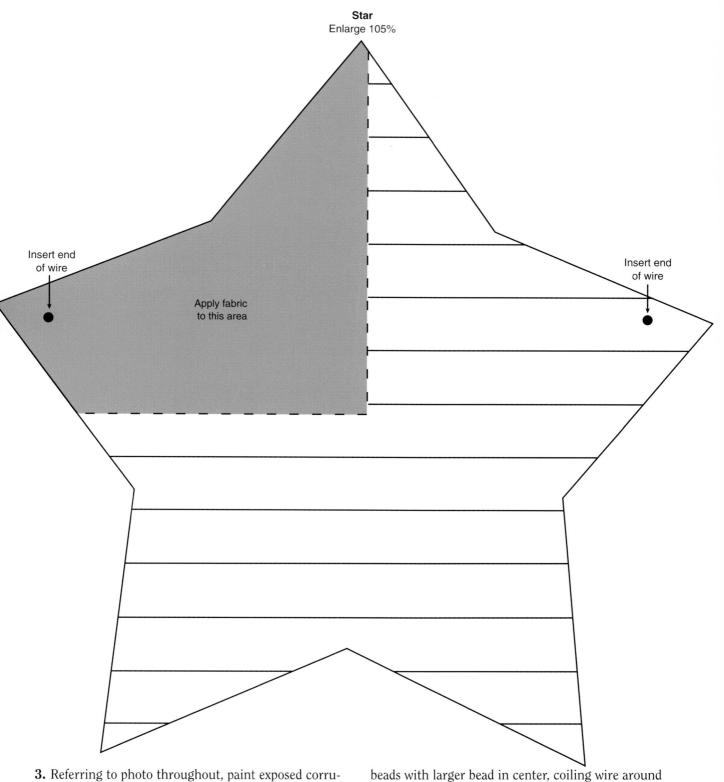

Star
Enlarge 105%

Insert end
of wire

Apply fabric
to this area

Insert end
of wire

3. Referring to photo throughout, paint exposed corrugated area with alternating horizontal red and white stripes. Let dry completely.

4. Press adhesive to wrong side of fabric square. Cut fabric to fit unpainted area of star; remove backing on adhesive and press in place.

5. Paint heart beads red; let dry. Insert wire through beads with larger bead in center, coiling wire around pencil to add extra shape and to secure beads along wire. Insert ends of wire through star where noted; twist ends to secure.

6. Cut raffia into three 1-yard pieces. Holding raffia and fabric strip together, tie onto wire in a bow. ★

—*Design by Janna Britton*

Patriotic Trio

Ready-made ribbon in patriotic colors and patterns makes it so simple to whip up a bundle of home dec accents just perfect for your Independence Day celebration.

Materials

Votive Holder

- 2½ yards 2¾"-wide America ribbon from Lion Ribbon Company
- ¼ yard ½"-wide red, white and blue striped ribbon
- ½"-thick sheet plastic foam
- Large square white felt
- White Curly Hair doll hair from One & Only Creations
- Hot-glue gun with needle-nose nozzle
- 1 white pearl spray
- 5 red floral heads
- White plastic milk or juice jug
- 2"-diameter clear glass votive

candle holder with white candle
- Lightweight sandpaper
- Craft knife or other cutting tool

Rocket Napkin Ring

- Cardboard tube from roll of paper towels or bathroom tissue
- Scraps of 2¾"-wide America ribbon from Lion Ribbon Company
- Scraps of white felt
- Craft glue

Door Decoration

- 3⅓ yards 2¾"-wide America ribbon from Lion Ribbon Company
- ⅔ yard ½"-wide red, white and blue striped ribbon

- ½"-thick sheet plastic foam
- Large square white felt
- White Curly Hair doll hair from One & Only Creations
- Hot-glue gun with needle-nose nozzle
- 1 white pearl spray
- 7 red floral heads on stems
- 7 blue floral heads on stems
- 1" diameter metal ring
- Lightweight sandpaper
- Craft knife or other cutting tool

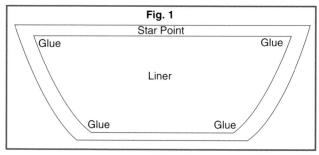

Instructions

Votive Candle Holder

1. Referring to patterns (page 99), cut 4" circle candle ring base from felt and plastic foam; lightly sand edges of plastic foam base. Glue felt to one side of plastic foam (this becomes bottom); set aside.

2. Cut 10 star points from America ribbon (position stars on ribbon along wider edge as shown) and 10 liners from white felt; glue a felt piece centered to the wrong side of each ribbon piece, applying glue to four "corners" of liner as shown in Fig. 1.

Fig. 1
Star Point
Glue · Glue
Liner
Glue · Glue

3. Fold and glue each star point as shown in Fig. 2 and Fig. 3.

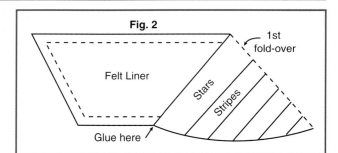

Fig. 2
Felt Liner
Stars
Stripes
1st fold-over
Glue here

4. Following numbers 1–5 in Fig. 4 (page 98), glue one side of base of each of five star points to top of plastic foam base, overlapping bottoms of points to fit.

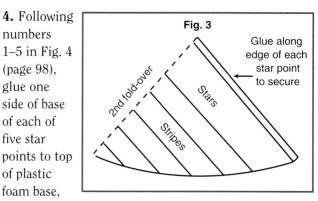

Fig. 3
2nd fold-over
Stripes
Stars
Glue along edge of each star point to secure

5. Following numbers 6–10 in Fig. 5 (page 98), open up

Continued on page 98

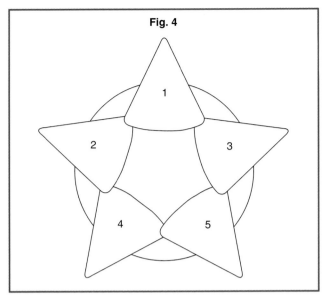

Fig. 4

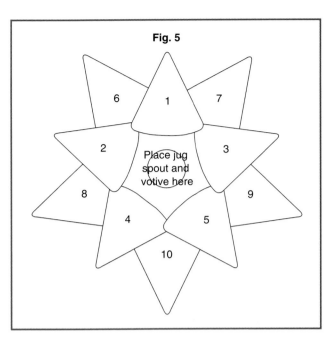

Fig. 5

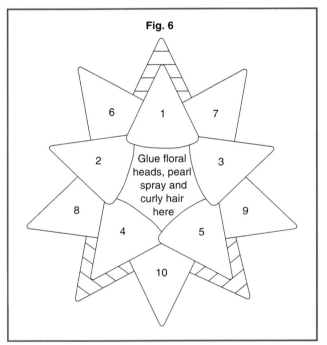

Fig. 6

base of each of five star points and glue edges to top and bottom of plastic foam base *between* points already glued in place, overlapping to fit.

6. Evenly cut a ¾"-tall piece including spout from top of plastic jug; glue base of spout to center of ring.

7. Knead a handful of doll hair with fingers to soften. Apply glue to plastic foam around jug spout. Press hair in place.

8. Cut heads from floral stems. Glue between bottoms of points in top row as shown.

9. Glue one end of each pearl strand to base of each star point in bottom row as shown.

10. Glue ribbon around base of votive candle holder. Set atop jug spout. Light candle. ***Note:*** *Never leave burning candle unattended.*

Rocket Napkin Ring

1. For each napkin ring, cut a 1¼"-wide section from cardboard tube.

2. Cut 6" x 1¼" section from striped portion of ribbon; wrap around cardboard ring, overlapping ends and trimming excess. Glue.

3. Cut one 1"-diameter star from remaining star-print portion of ribbon and one star from felt. Glue felt to wrong side of ribbon star; glue other side of felt to center of napkin ring.

4. Gather paper or fabric napkin in center and pull through napkin ring to form "rocket."

Door Decoration

1. Referring to patterns (page 99), cut candle ring base

from felt and plastic foam; lightly sand edges of plastic foam base.

2. Cut 12" piece of ½"-wide ribbon; glue around edge of base, overlapping ends and trimming excess.

3. Cut 13 star points from America ribbon (position stars on ribbon along wider edge as shown) and 13 liners from white felt; glue a felt piece centered to the wrong side of each ribbon piece, applying glue to four "corners" of liner as shown in Fig. 1 (page 96).

4. Fold each star point as shown in Fig. 2 and Fig. 3 (page 96).

Star Points
Cut 10 from America ribbon,
positioning stars at top as shown

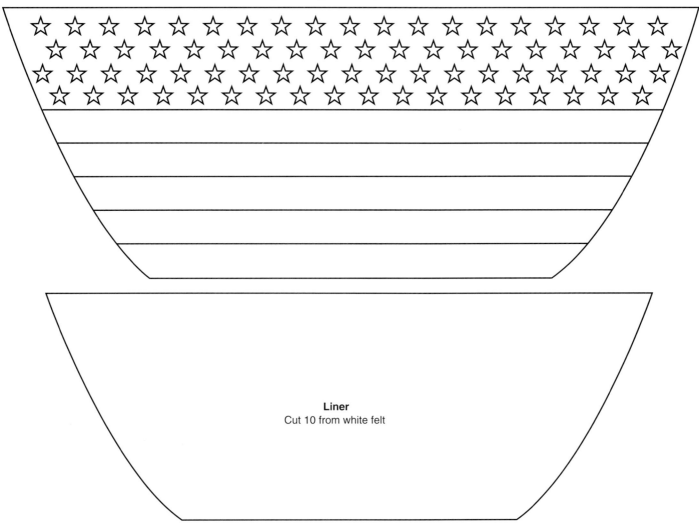

Liner
Cut 10 from white felt

5. Following numbers 1–5 in Fig. 4, glue one side of base of each of five star points to top of plastic foam base, overlapping to fit.

6. Following numbers 6–10 in Fig. 5, open base of each of five star points and glue edges to top and bottom of plastic foam base *between* points already glued in place, overlapping bottoms of points to fit.

7. Following numbers 11–13 in Fig. 6, glue remaining points behind points 1, 4 and 5.

8. Knead a handful of doll hair with fingers to soften. Apply glue to plastic foam in center. Press hair in place.

9. Trim floral stems to 2" in length; glue randomly to center of ring.

10. Separate pearl strands and glue them randomly among floral heads.

11. Cut 12" piece of ½"-wide red, white and blue ribbon; fold in half and slip ring to middle of ribbon. Glue ends to back of base.

12. Glue felt circle to back of decoration to finish. ★

—*Designs by Joanna Randolph Rott*

Patriotic Wind Sock

Fly the national colors with pride this Fourth of July and all year long with this colorful wind sock!

Materials

- 10" metal ring
- 1¾ yards blue-and-white ticking or other striped fabric
- ⅜ yard each of 4 patriotic fabrics including stars, stripes and flags (see Project Notes)
- ⅓ yard navy-and-white star print fabric
- 1 yard Wonder Under fusible webbing by Pellon
- 1 yard thin craft batting
- 18" ¼"-wide navy blue satin ribbon
- 1 package blue star sequins
- 1 package tiny gold beads
- 10" heavy nylon thread
- 1 spool metallic gold thread
- 1 spool light blue sewing thread
- Lightweight cardboard
- Rubber cement
- Sewing machine with walking foot and open-toe foot

Project Notes

Sample project was completed using a red-and-white striped fabric, an American flag print novelty fabric that coordinates with the star print, red fabric with gold pin dots and blue fabric with gold pin dots.

Use ¼" seam allowance throughout.

Instructions

1. Prewash and dry all fabrics, using no fabric softener.

2. From blue-and-white striped fabric, cut two panels 11¼" x 24½" and one backing piece 24½" x 32". From star print, cut four strips 2" x 32". From the assorted fabrics, cut a total of seven strips, each 24½" long and ranging in width from 1½"–2½"; combined widths of two panels and seven strips when sewn together should equal 32".

3. Trace stars for striped panels of wind sock onto back of fusible webbing (on our project, a total of one large, five medium and four small stars were used). Fuse webbing

Continued on page 103

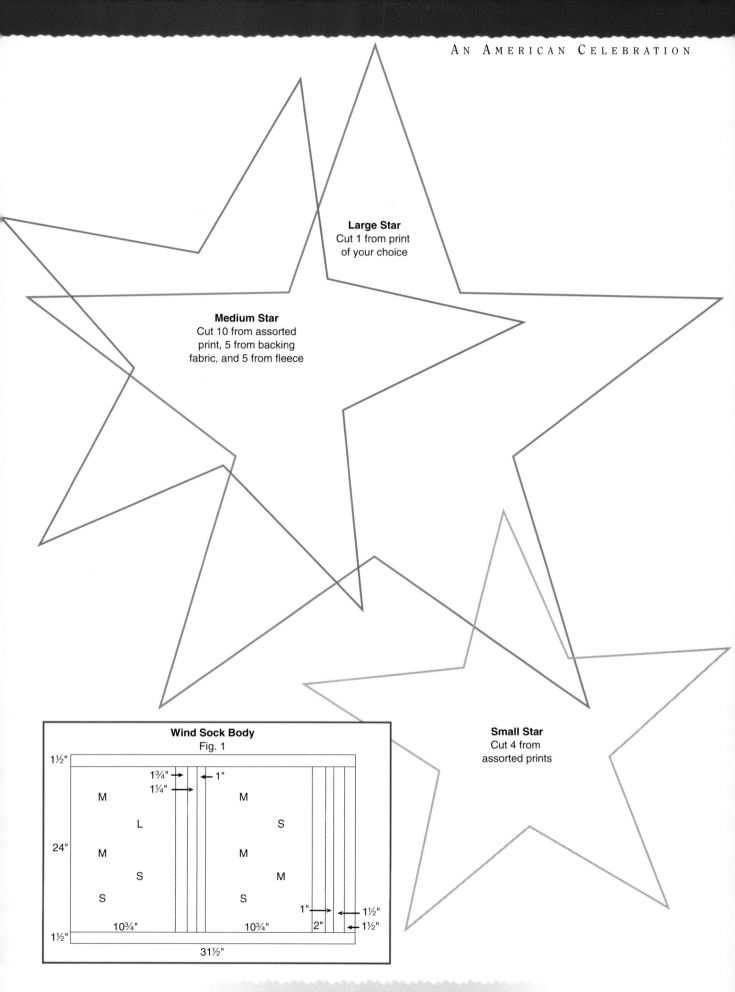

Large Star
Cut 1 from print
of your choice

Medium Star
Cut 10 from assorted
print, 5 from backing
fabric, and 5 from fleece

Small Star
Cut 4 from
assorted prints

Wind Sock Body
Fig. 1

1½"

1¾" →
1¼" →

← 1"

M

M

L

S

24"

M

M

S

M

S

S

1" →

← 1½"

2"

← 1½"

1½"

10¾"

10¾"

31½"

Cowboy & Cowgirl Dolls

*Whip up these cute dolls in a jiffy—they're perfect favors or
table decorations for your next summer barbecue or family reunion.*

Materials

- 2 Forster, Inc., wooden doll pins
- 2 Forster, Inc., wooden head beads
- 2 (1³⁄₁₆"-wide) wooden hearts
- 2 (3") straw hats
- 2 (2¼" x 3¼") pieces old denim
- Red-and-white gingham:
  3" x 10" strip
  5½" x ⅝" strip
  4½" square
- 7" ¼"-wide red satin ribbon
- 2" ⅛"-wide red satin ribbon
- Acrylic paints: skin tone, burnt umber, white and red
- Black extra-fine–point permanent marking pen
- Creme cosmetic blusher
- ¼" flat paintbrush
- #1 liner brush
- Toothpick
- Low-temperature glue gun
- Sewing machine
- White sewing thread
- 2" brown acrylic hair fiber
- 3 yards natural jute twine
- ³⁄₁₆"-diameter wooden dowel
- Masking tape

Instructions

1. Base-coat both head beads with skin-tone paint and flat paintbrush; let dry. With finger, lightly apply creme blusher to cheeks.

2. Referring to photo throughout, use wooden end of liner brush to dot on eyes with burnt umber. With burnt umber add both noses, and cowboy's eyebrows and smile. Let dry.

3. Add cowgirl's lips with red and tiny white highlight dots to both dolls' eyes. Let dry. Carefully add cowgirl's eyelashes with extra-fine marking pen.

4. Wrap each doll pin with a piece of denim; glue closed at overlap; overlap will be at back of doll.

5. Glue head beads onto dolls.

6. Paint one heart red and one burnt umber; let dry. Glue red heart to base of girl doll for feet, "cheeks" of heart facing forward. Glue burnt umber heart to cowboy.

7. Referring to pattern, cut scarf from gingham square. Tie tightly around boy's neck with knot in back; trim off excess.

Scarf
Cut 1 from gingham square

8. Glue acrylic hair to cowboy's head. Fold narrower gingham strip in half lengthwise; wrap around hat crown and glue. Fold hat sides up; glue in place to resemble cowboy hat. Glue hat to head. Trim cowboy's hair.

9. Using white thread, zigzag one long edge of wider gingham strip for skirt hem. Fold top edge under ½"; baste ¼" from fold and gather. Pull gathers to fit around cowgirl's waist. Glue skirt onto cowgirl with seam at back; glue seam closed. Wrap ⅛" red ribbon around waist, overlapping ends in back. Trim off excess ribbon.

10. Wrap jute tightly around dowel; tape ends to hold in place. Dampen jute lightly with water; let dry. Untape ends and slide jute off dowel. Cut jute into 6" pieces; separate strands.

11. Glue jute strands to center of cowgirl's head so hair falls down sides of head. Cut short curls for bangs; glue in place.

12. Glue ¼" red ribbon around hat brim, overlapping ends in back and leaving 1" ribbon tails. Glue sides of hat brim up. Glue hat to cowgirl's head. ★

—*Designs by Janna Britton*

Patriotic Windsock

Continued from page 100

stars to the ⅜-yard cuts of fabric. Cut out. Fuse stars to panels (see Fig. 1, page 101, for suggested layout).

4. Referring to Fig. 1 (page 101), join panels and assorted 24½"-long strips.

5. Lay backing fabric facedown on work surface; top with batting, then pieced top, right side up. Pin to hold layers securely.

6. Using gold metallic thread, machine-appliqué around stars and satin-stitch along some of the seams of the assorted stripes.

7. Using light blue thread and walking foot on sewing machine, quilt angular lines, some radiating from the stars, over striped panels.

8. Stitch two 2" x 32" strips together along one long edge, with right sides facing; repeat with remaining two strips. Finger-press seams open. Sew one strip set to top of quilted piece and the other to bottom, right sides facing.

9. Attach sequins and beads randomly over striped surface: Thread needle and knot thread; bring needle up

from back; slip sequin, then bead over needle; insert needle back through sequin and fabric. Knot off on wrong side. Bring thread up at next point of attachment without puckering fabric.

10. Place side edges of quilted piece together, right sides facing; sew seam. Finger-press seam open. Place metal ring at top, positioning on seam line between two top strips on wrong side. Fold top strip down, encasing ring. Whipstitch ring into place. Fold under seam allowance; hand-stitch, enclosing all seam allowances.

11. Turn bottom facing to wrong side; fold in seam allowance and hand-stitch, enclosing all seam allowances.

12. Make hanger by attaching ribbon ends opposite each other inside top of wind sock. Attach loop of heavy nylon thread to ribbon so wind sock can twirl freely.

13. Using medium star pattern, cut five each print fabric backing and batting. Layer a star of backing fabric and a star of print fabric, right sides facing; top each with batting star. Stitch perimeter, leaving opening for turning. Turn star right side out; hand-stitch openings closed. Tack stars at even intervals around base of wind sock. ★

—*Design by Charlyne Stewart*

Patriotic Tree

*Curly ribbon lets you make a festive decoration for your
holiday picnic or family reunion in under two hours!*

Materials

- 7" terra cotta flowerpot with saucer
- 2-part epoxy or craft cement
- Woodsies wooden stars from Forster's Mfg.: ⅞", 1³⁄₁₆" and 1⅝" wide
- Aluminum foil
- Plaster of paris or sand
- Small branch with slender twigs
- Red shredded paper
- 3 yards 2½"-wide wire-edge ribbon in patriotic colors
- Curling ribbon: red, white and blue
- Low-temperature glue gun
- Thin white fabric-wrapped wire
- 4½" x 3" piece thin white cardboard
- Acrylic paints: blue and red
- White spray paint
- Gold webbing spray paint
- White dimensional paint
- Paintbrush
- Small checkerboard stencil or checkerboard stamp cut from sponge

Instructions

1. Wash flowerpot and saucer; dry completely.

2. Glue flowerpot to saucer with epoxy or cement. Let dry.

3. Paint pot, saucer, branch and stars with white spray paint; let dry. Apply a second coat if necessary for good coverage. Spray stars with gold webbing spray paint, if desired.

4. Place a wad of aluminum foil in bottom of flowerpot to cover hole. Mix plaster of paris; stand branch in flowerpot and fill pot at least half-full with plaster of paris. Let harden undisturbed.

5. Cover top of plaster with shredded paper.

6. Referring to photo throughout, wrap wire-edge ribbon around pot; glue ends to secure. With remaining ribbon, form a bow with three loops on each side; glue or wire over ribbon.

7. Cut lengths of red, white and blue curling ribbons; holding a strand of each color together, curl ribbon over scissors. Tie curled clusters around branches and twigs.

Fourth of July Napkin Rings

Whip these up in minutes for your Independence Day picnic!

Materials

Each Napkin Ring

- Craft foam:

  2" x 6" strip blue

  2" x 3" piece white

- 2" x 3⅜" piece cut from double-sided adhesive sheet

- Jesse James & Co. novelty buttons:

  7–8 (⅝") red hearts

  1" flag or flag heart

- Tacky craft glue

Instructions

1. Trim 2" x ⅜" strip from adhesive piece; set aside. Fuse remaining 2" x 3" adhesive to one side of white craft foam. Cut white foam into 2"-long strips of random widths. Peel off paper backing; referring to Fig. 1, press white strips onto blue napkin ring.

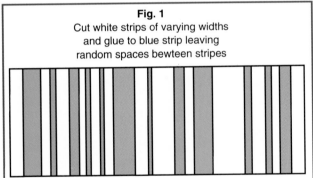

Fig. 1
Cut white strips of varying widths
and glue to blue strip leaving
random spaces bewteen stripes

2. Referring to photo, glue buttons to napkin ring. Let dry thoroughly.

3. Fuse 2" x ⅜" strip adhesive to back of napkin ring along one short end. Peel off adhesive backing; fuse to other end of blue foam to form ring. Press firmly. ★

—*Design by Judi Kauffman*

Patriotic Tree

Continued from page 104

8. Cut one 12"–14" length of thin wire for every two stars. Glue one star to each end of wire, reserving a large star for flag; coil wire around pencil. Wrap wired stars around tree branches.

9. Paint upper left corner of cardboard blue to resemble blue field on a flag; stamp rest of "flag" in a checkerboard pattern of red over the white background; let dry. Outline flag and blue field with white dimensional paint; let dry. Glue one of the largest stars in the center of the blue field; let dry. Coil another strand of white wire; glue both ends to back of flag, and loop over tree branch. ★

—*Design by Beth Wheeler*

Tricks & Treats

Delight your little ghosts and goblins by dressing up your Halloween home with lots of spooky decorations, and by adding handmade accents to the scariest of costumes! Party accents, Halloween masks, table sets and much more will make your Halloween house the most popular one on the block!

Haunted House

*This cute country cottage has a few unauthorized tenants for the Halloween season—
a row of jack-o'-lanterns outside, a whimsical witch with candy-corn "wings"
floating above the roof, and a UFO—that's "unidentified frightening object"—
peering from the window. What a cute addition to your cozy abode!*

Materials

- Aleene's Enhancers paints and finishes:
  All-Purpose Primer #EN 104
  Matté Varnish #EN 107
- Aleene's Essentials acrylic paints:
  Ivory #OC 179
  Blush #OC 183
  Yellow ochre #OC 184
  Burnt umber #OC 185
- Aleene's Premium-Coat Acrylics paint:

True orange #OC 115
Medium yellow #OC 126
Deep sage #OC 134
Black #OC 176
- ¾" flat brush
- #10/0 liner brush
- Spatter brush
- Stylus
- Thick tacky craft glue
- Expandable sponge
- 6 craft sticks
- 3½" doll body from Lara's Crafts

- Drill
- Wooden house from Lara's Crafts
- Jute twine
- Needle-nose pliers
- Poster board
- Primitive wooden star shape from Lara's Crafts
- Sandpaper
- Fence wire
- Wire cutters

Project Note

Refer to photo throughout for color placement.

Instructions

1. Mix equal parts primer and water. Using ¾" flat brush, apply one coat to house; let dry. Sand lightly.

2. Thin burnt umber to a milky consistency to create a stain. Using flat brush, apply stain to house and craft sticks.

3. Using flat brush, paint base deep sage. Let dry; sand edges.

4. Using flat brush and medium yellow, paint 1½" square for window and paint wooden star shape; let dry. Paint over window and star with yellow ochre; let dry. Sand edges of star. Using ¾" flat brush, paint shutters deep sage. Paint edge of roof and roofline on front of house burnt umber.

5. Referring to patterns, trace shapes for leaf, ghost and jack-o'-lantern onto expandable sponge, tracing body of jack-o'-lantern and stem as separate shapes; cut out and immerse in water to expand. Wring out excess water.

6. Using flat brush, paint surface of ghost sponge with ivory paint; press into the window area. Paint jack-o'-lantern sponge with true orange; sponge three across

bottom of house. Paint stem sponge with burnt umber; sponge stems atop jack-o'-lanterns. Paint leaf sponge deep sage and paint edge of sponge yellow ochre; press atop pumpkins.

7. Thin black paint with water to inky consistency. Using liner brush, create shingles on house by painting wiggly lines horizontally across house about ¾" apart; stagger vertical lines to give a bricked effect.

8. Using flat brush, shade left side of each shingle with burnt umber. Dip brush handle in black to make two dots on the right side of each shingle. ***Hint:** Re-dip after each dot so they will be uniform in size.*

9. Using stylus, dot black eyes onto ghost.

10. Thin black with water to inky consistency. Using liner brush, paint eyes, noses and mouths on pumpkins and ghost's mouth; outline the roof, leaves, ghost, window, shutters, tendrils on pumpkin and bow around ghost's neck. Using thinned black paint, lightly spatter house and base.

11. Using flat brush, base-coat witch's dress black. Referring to patten, cut witch's hat from poster board. Using flat brush, paint hat black and witch's face blush. Using stylus, dot eyes with black.

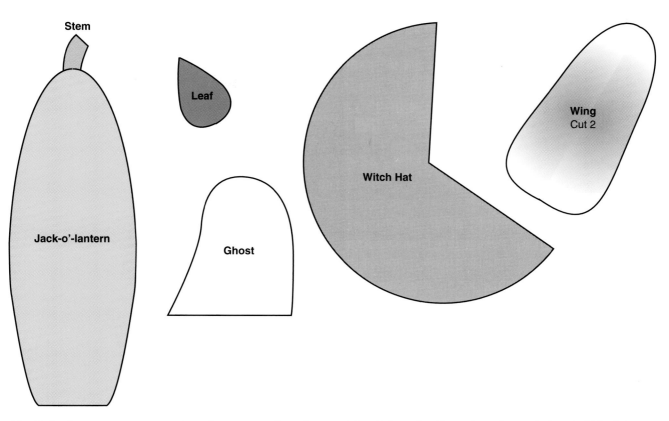

Stem

Leaf

Wing
Cut 2

Witch Hat

Jack-o'-lantern

Ghost

12. Referring to pattern, cut wings from poster board. Using the ¾" flat brush, paint wings like candy corn: large ends with true orange, centers ivory and small ends medium yellow. Lightly spatter wings with thinned black; let dry.

13. Drill hole in each side of witch's body. Using needle-nose pliers, coil and kink two pieces of wire, leaving ends straight. Glue one end in each hole; glue wings to other ends of wires.

14. Glue 3½" strands of jute twine across top of witch's head; unravel. Glue painted hat into cone shape; glue hat to head. Tie bow from a single strand of jute; glue to witch's neck.

15. Kink and coil another piece of wire. Drill hole in bottom of witch; glue one end of wire in hole.

16. Cut craft sticks in half; sand edges. Beginning at bottom of roof edge on right side, glue craft stick pieces in place for shingles, overlapping by about half. Repeat on other side.

17. Drill hole in left side of roof; insert other end of witch's wire. Glue star to house; tie bow from jute twine and glue to star.

18. Using ¾" flat brush, apply one or two coats matte varnish to painted surfaces. ◆

—Design by Bonnie Stephens for Duncan Enterprises

Pumpkin T-Shirt

*Don't just set a jack-o'-lantern on your doorstep this Halloween—
wear one, too! This happy jack comes to life courtesy of your scrap bag.*

Materials

- 2 orange print fabrics
- Dark olive print fabric
- Light olive print fabric
- Gold solid fabric
- Fusible webbing
- Sewing threads: orange, black and green
- Seam sealant
- 2 ($7/16$") black buttons
- 14" $5/8$"-wide green grosgrain ribbon

Instructions

1. Prewash and dry T-shirt and fabrics using no fabric softener. Following manufacturer's instructions, fuse webbing to backs of all fabrics.

2. Referring to photo and patterns, cut letters from one of the orange prints and pumpkin from the other, stem from light olive, leaves from dark olive, and eyes, mouth and nose from gold.

3. Fold T-shirt in half to find center line down front; mark center with pins or basting thread.

4. Referring to photo for placement, fuse eyes, nose and mouth to pumpkin. Fuse pumpkin to shirt. Using black thread, machine-appliqué eyes, nose and mouth; using orange, machine-appliqué pumpkin.

5. Fuse stem to T-shirt; machine-appliqué with green thread.

6. Fuse leaves onto shirt; machine-appliqué around edges and down centers with green thread.

7. Fuse letters onto shirt; machine-appliqué with orange thread.

8. Sew black buttons onto eyes.

9. Tie 3" bow with ribbon; trim streamers to about 1½" and coat edges with seam sealant; let dry. Sew bow to base of pumpkin stem. ◆

—Design by Helen L. Rafson

Pumpkin Shirt
Enlarge 130%

Scarecrow Pin

Give your wardrobe a seasonal boost with this brightly painted wooden pin. Raffia hair gives him the homespun charm of a real scarecrow.

Materials

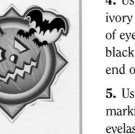

- ⅛"-thick birch plywood or other thin stock
- Scroll saw or small hand saw
- Sandpaper
- Wood sealer
- Ceramcoat acrylic paints by Delta Technical Coatings: rosetta, tangerine, yellow, maple sugar, burnt sienna, adobe, black and ivory
- Paintbrushes:
  #8 shader
  #1 liner
  #10/0 liner
- Ultra-fine permanent black marking pen
- Artist's pastel stick in deep madder or cosmetic blusher
- Raffia: natural and green
- Wood glue
- Clamp
- Krylon acrylic matté sealer #1311
- 1" pin back
- Craft cement
- Tiny fabric scrap

Instructions

1. Referring to patterns, cut pieces from birch plywood using scroll saw, cutting head and crown as one piece. Sand edges until smooth. Give all pieces a coat of wood sealer; let dry and sand again.

2. Referring to patterns and photo, paint back of large piece, sides, crown and outer edges of brim area using #8 shader brush and maple sugar. Do not paint back of brim piece. Paint face with rosetta; paint collar with tangerine. Shade edges of brim and hat indentation with burnt sienna.

3. Using #10/0 liner and adobe, paint stitching line down center of face. Using #1 liner, paint nose with adobe; paint yellow stripes on collar; paint black eyes. Let dry.

4. Using #1 liner brush, paint ivory circles over black portions of eyes; when dry, dot on black pupils using end of stylus.

5. Using ultra-fine marking pen, add eyelashes and mouth. Add blush to the cheeks using pastel stick or blusher.

6. Cut several uneven 1"-1½" pieces of natural raffia and a few ½" pieces. Spread wood glue on brim area of pin; position raffia for hair and bangs, taking care not to make them too even. Spread wood glue on back of brim and position over raffia on pin, adjusting raffia as necessary. Clamp pieces together tightly; let dry.

7. Cut tiny piece of fabric for patch; glue to brim. Tie 1½" bow from green raffia; glue to pin.

8. Spray pin with two light coats of acrylic sealer; let dry. Using craft cement, attach pin back. ◆

—*Design by Ginger Miller*

Scarecrow Pin

112

Pumpkin Pin

This jack-o'-lantern's snaggle-tooth grin is sure to bring smiles this fall. He's lightweight, and quick to paint.

Instructions

1. Referring to pattern, cut shape from birch plywood using scroll saw. Sand wood until edges and surface are smooth. Coat with wood sealer; let dry and sand again.

2. Using #8 shader, base-coat pin with pumpkin; let dry.

3. Using #1 liner, paint stem and leaf with hunter green; shade base of stem and leaf center with black. Paint mouth and eyes black; let dry.

4. Using #1 liner, paint white circles on eyes and paint teeth over mouth. When dry, dot on pupils with stylus tip dipped in black.

5. Using ultra-fine marking pen, add eyelashes and grin lines.

6. When all paints and ink are thoroughly dry, rub a little of pastel stick onto sandpaper or other paper. Using old worn paintbrush, brush in cheek color.

Materials

- ⅛"-thick birch plywood or other thin stock
- Scroll saw or small hand saw
- Sandpaper
- Wood sealer
- Ceramcoat acrylic paints by Delta Technical Coatings: pumpkin, hunter green, black and white
- Paintbrushes:
  #8 shader
  #1 liner
- Old worn artist's paintbrush
- Ultra-fine permanent black marking pen
- Carmine artist's pastel stick
- Krylon matté acrylic spray sealer #1311
- 1" pin back
- Craft cement

7. Spray pin with two light coats of acrylic sealer; let dry. Using craft cement, attach pin back. ◆

—Design by Ginger Miller

Pumpkin Pin

Halloween Tree

Win compliments when you arrange your Halloween party treats around this wonderfully creepy centerpiece! Ghosts and bats float among its scraggly limbs— and we don't know "whooo!" owns all those eyes peering from the branches!

Materials

- 20" vine tree
- Spanish moss
- STYROFOAM® plastic foam:
  12" x 36" x ½" sheet
  2" ball
  2 (1½") balls
  2 (1¼") balls
- 3¼" x 4½" section wooden picket fence
- Flat black spray paint
- Dimensional fabric paints: black, white and bright green
- Acrylic paints: black, yellow, white and bright green
- ⅜"-wide grosgrain ribbon:
  1¾ yards black
  1⅞ yards white
  ¼ yard yellow
- ⅛"-wide double-face satin ribbon:
  ⅞ yard orange
  1½ yards black
- 2" square poster board
- Fabric:
  ⅛ yard orange
  ⅛ yard black
  ¼ yard white
  2 (5") squares black pin dot
  2 (3¼") squares bright yellow
- 5 (½") pieces ⅛"-diameter dowel rod
- Thick and thin white craft glues
- Glow-in-the-dark multicolored glitter
- ¾" flat paintbrush
- Low-temperature glue gun
- Round toothpicks
- Awl
- Cookie cutters: ghost, bat, cat and 2⅝" round
- Straight pins

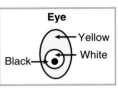

Project Notes

Refer to photo throughout for construction and placement.

Use thick craft glue applied with a toothpick except where noted otherwise.

Tree

1. Lightly spray tree with black spray paint. Let dry.

2. Separate Spanish moss into small strands; glue onto tree branches.

Figures & Eyes

1. Using cookie cutters as patterns throughout, cut three bats, five ghosts, one cat and one round from ½"-thick plastic foam sheet. Cut same number of shapes from *doubled* layers of fabric, adding ¼" seam allowance and using black fabric for bats, white for ghosts, black pin dot for cat and yellow for round.

2. Separate pairs of fabric shapes; center fabric cutouts over both sides of plastic foam shape and hold in place with pins. Clip seam allowance at ¼" intervals; glue tabs to edges of shapes.

3. Cut matching colors of grosgrain ribbon to fit around each shape allowing ½" overlap; glue in place, positioning seam in most inconspicuous place.

4. Referring to pattern, cut 10 eyes from poster board; paint yellow; let dry. Paint white circle; let dry. Add black highlight dot with toothpick; let dry.

Eye
Yellow
White
Black

5. Apply coat of thin glue to fronts of eyes, bats and ghosts; sprinkle with glitter. Let dry.

6. Add facial features with dimensional fabric paints: bright green dot eye to cat, black eyes and smiles to ghosts, and white eyes and smiles to bats.

7. Cut three 6" lengths from orange satin ribbon; tie each in bow and trim ends at angle. Glue one to each bat. Tie 10" length of orange ribbon around cat's neck.

8. Cut five 6" lengths from black satin ribbon; tie each in bow and trim ends at angle. Glue one to each ghost.

9. Using flat paintbrush, paint fence white; let dry.

Pumpkins

1. Paint dowel pieces with bright green acrylic paint for stems; let dry.

2. Cut seven ½"-wide strips and four ¼"-wide strips from orange fabric, cutting from selvage to selvage. Applying glue only to ends of strips, wrap 2" and 1½" balls with ½" strips, and other balls with ¼" strips.

3. Using awl, punch hole in top of each pumpkin. Apply glue to end of each stem; press into pumpkins.

Assembly

1. Glue one bat to moon.

2. Cut three 6" pieces black satin ribbon. Using awl, make holes in tops of moon and two ghosts. Fold ribbon pieces in half; glue center of ribbon in hole; tie figures to branches.

3. Using hot-glue gun, glue cat and two pumpkins to fence. Arrange remaining shapes and pairs of eyes and glue in place on and around tree. ◆

—Design by Annabelle Keller

Halloween Masks

Reintroduce your family to the fun of making your own Halloween outfits! These colorful masks are soft and comfy foam. You can tie them to fit with ribbon and cut the eye openings as large as you want, making them very safe alternatives to molded plastic masks, which can slide all over the face.

Materials

Monster

- Craft foam: black and lime green
- Scribbles 3-Dimensional Fabric Writers by Duncan Enterprises:
  Fluorescent neon orange
  Fluorescent neon yellow
  Iridescent blush red
- Craft glue
- 1 yard ¼"-wide white satin ribbon

Cat

- Black craft foam
- Scribbles 3-Dimensional Fabric Writers by Duncan Enterprises:
  Fluorescent neon orange
  Fluorescent neon green
- Craft glue
- 1 yard ¼"-wide white satin ribbon

Pumpkin

- Orange craft foam
- Scribbles 3-Dimensional Fabric Writers by Duncan Enterprises:
  Fluorescent neon green
  Fluorescent neon yellow
- Craft glue
- 1 yard ¼"-wide white satin ribbon

Instructions

Monster

1. Referring to patterns, cut hair from black craft foam and head from lime green. Check position of eye holes to make sure vision will be unobstructed.

2. Glue hair to face; let dry.

3. Referring to patterns and photo, add details with three-dimensional paint: Outline hair with neon orange; draw nose, "scars" and ear bolts with blush red; outline eyes and remainder of face and add nostrils with neon yellow; let dry completely.

4. Cut ribbon in half. Glue one end of each piece to center of each side on back of mask, using a generous amount of glue for a secure hold.

Pumpkin

1. Referring to pattern, cut pumpkin mask from orange craft foam. Check position of eye holes to make sure vision will be unobstructed.

2. Referring to pattern and photo, add details with three-dimensional paint: Outline nose and draw stem with neon green; outline eyes and remainder of face with neon yellow; let dry completely.

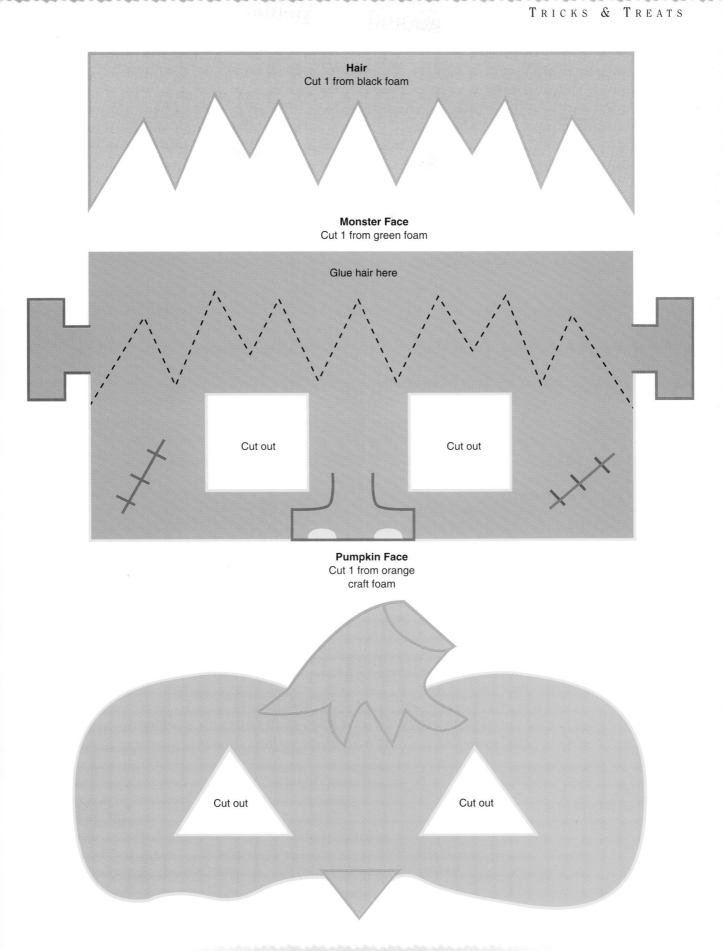

Hair
Cut 1 from black foam

Monster Face
Cut 1 from green foam

Glue hair here

Cut out

Cut out

Pumpkin Face
Cut 1 from orange
craft foam

Cut out

Cut out

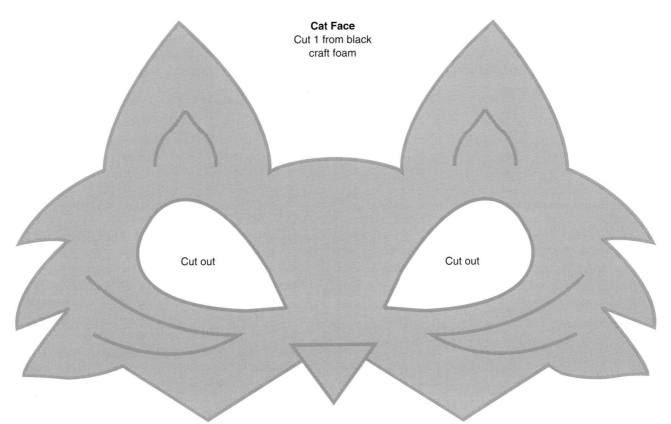

Cat Face
Cut 1 from black
craft foam

Cut out

Cut out

3. Cut ribbon in half. Glue one end of each piece to center of each side on back of mask, using a generous amount of glue for a secure hold.

Cat

1. Referring to pattern, cut cat's face from black craft foam. Check position of eye holes to make sure vision will be unobstructed.

2. Referring to pattern and photo, add details with three-dimensional paint: Outline eyes and nose and draw whiskers and inner ears with neon green; outline remainder of face with neon orange; let dry completely.

3. Cut ribbon in half. Glue one end of each piece to center of each side on back of mask, using a generous amount of glue for a secure hold. ◆

—*Designs by Mary T. Cosgrove*

Halloween Friends

Present this pair of molded Halloween buddies to extra-special trick-or-treaters.
They're just the right size to perch on a shelf, or in one of the cubbyholes
of an old typesetter's tray, along with other miniatures of the season.

Materials
- Sculpey III modeling compound by Polyform:
  Green #022
  Orange #032
  Black #042
  Red #082
- Flesh #092
- 4 black seed beads
- Straight-edge tool for cutting and making lines
- Plastic canvas yarn in desired color for hair
- 1½" broom
- Craft glue
- Hot-glue gun
- Straight pin
- Round toothpick

Project Notes

Refer to photo for placement of various components.

Modeling even the tiniest pieces for designs like this is much easier if you first take a moment to soften the modeling compound between your fingers. Remember to always cleanse your hands thoroughly when switching colors.

Instructions

1. For witch's body, cut off a quarter-section of black modeling compound; soften between your hands and roll into a ball. Shape ball into a cone; stand flat end on work surface.

2. Soften and work a marble-size ball of flesh modeling compound for face. Press onto tip of cone. Referring to Fig. 1, press two black seed beads on their sides into head for eyes; press just until none of the bead hole shows. Rub the tip of your little finger into red modeling compound; transfer this color onto cheeks.

Fig. 1

3. Roll a tiny ball of flesh modeling compound for nose; add smile, eyelashes and eyebrows with straight pin.

4. To make hat brim, roll marble-size ball of black compound into a 1½" rope of even thickness, rolling the ball back and forth on work surface. Flatten rope; form into circular hat brim and press onto head; brim should not touch face and should be attached a little lower in the back. Cut off excess modeling compound when ends are joined.

5. Roll a cone of black compound and tilt tip a bit; attach flat base of cone to head and hat brim.

6. Roll two pea-size balls of compound, one of orange and one of black; roll into very thin ropes of equal size and thickness. Twist ropes together and attach around hat, trimming off excess.

7. Roll each of two marble-size balls of black compound into 1"-long arms; attach pea-size ball of flesh compound to end of each for hand. Attach other end of arm to body at shoulder only.

8. Cut a quarter-section from the orange compound. Cut this section in half and cut one of those halves in half. Cut one of the resulting halves in half again, giving you ⅛ of the original quarter-section. Soften, roll and shape into a tallish pumpkin shape.

Fig. 2

9. Referring to Fig. 2, press two black seed beads on their sides into head for eyes; press just until none of the bead hole shows. Roll a tiny ball of orange modeling compound for nose; add smile, eyelashes and eyebrows with straight pin. With round toothpick, make a hole in the top to accept the stem. With smooth straight edge, make vertical lines in pumpkin.

10. Make a cone shape from a tiny ball of green modeling compound for stem, sticking pointed end of cone into hole in top of pumpkin.

11. Form a ball of red half the size of a pea into a small half-circle for witch's foot; affix to bottom right at base of witch.

12. Set witch on ovenproof plate; position pumpkin next to witch with her hand resting on it. Test fit of broomstick in crook of other arm, but remove broom for now. Bake figure on ovenproof plate in preheated 275-degree oven for 10 minutes; let cool completely.

13. Cut nine ½"-long pieces of yarn for hair; glue them to witch using hot-glue gun, positioning three strands as bangs and three on each side of her face. Separate and fluff strands with a pin; trim as needed.

14. Glue broomstick in crook of arm. ◆

—Design by Jackie Haskell

Felt Halloween Pins

*Whip up a batch of these fun pins in next to no time! They work just as nicely
as magnets, or as tiny ornaments to dangle throughout your home.*

Materials

Cat
- 8" square black felt
- 2 (¼") black-and-white buttons
- 10" white #5 pearl cotton
- White 6-strand embroidery floss
- Sewer's beeswax
- 6mm half-round black cabochon
- Tacky craft glue
- Small amount fiberfill
- 1" pin back

Ghost
- 3" x 6" white felt
- Scrap of black felt
- Black 6-strand embroidery floss
- Tacky craft glue
- Small amount fiberfill
- 1" pin back

Pumpkin
- 3" x 6" pumpkin felt
- Scrap of black felt
- Scrap of kelly green felt

- Black fine-tip marker
- 6-strand embroidery floss: black and green
- Size 6 knitting needle
- Tape
- Tacky craft glue
- Small amount fiberfill
- 1" pin back

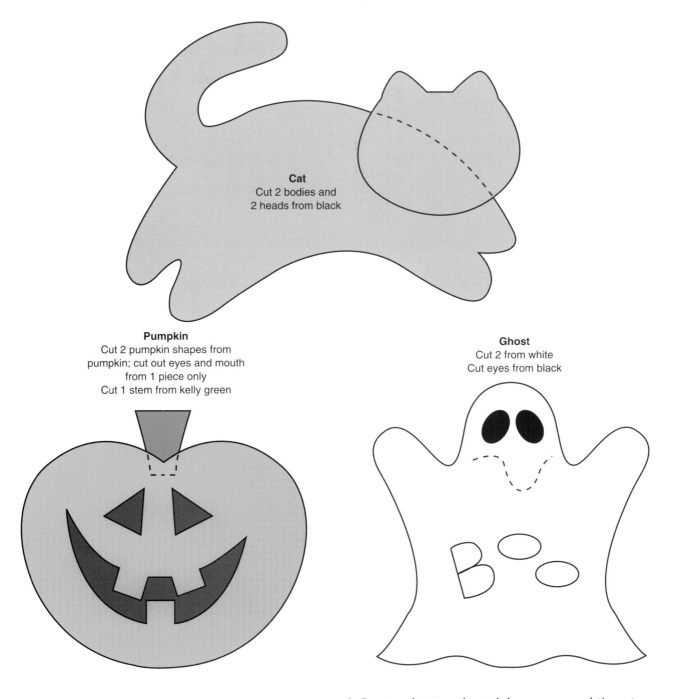

Cat
Cut 2 bodies and
2 heads from black

Pumpkin
Cut 2 pumpkin shapes from
pumpkin; cut out eyes and mouth
from 1 piece only
Cut 1 stem from kelly green

Ghost
Cut 2 from white
Cut eyes from black

Instructions

Cat

1. Referring to patterns, cut two cat bodies and two cat heads from black felt.

2. Pin body pieces together; join body pieces with Blanket Stitch using 2 strands white embroidery floss and leaving opening for stuffing. Stuff body lightly with fiberfill and Blanket Stitch opening closed.

3. Referring to photo, sew buttons to one head piece for eyes; sew and stuff head pieces as you did body pieces.

4. Run pearl cotton through beeswax several times to stiffen. Thread needle and run pearl cotton through center of face three times, clipping to leave 1" whiskers. Glue black cabochon over center of whiskers.

5. Glue head to body. Sew or glue pin back to back of cat.

Ghost

1. Referring to patterns, cut two ghosts from white felt and two eyes from black felt.

2. Referring to photo throughout, glue felt eyes to one

Continued on page 123

121

Fishbowl Treat Jar

Trick-or-treaters will have lots of fun fishing for treats from this clever container decorated with a jack-o'-lantern assembled from colorful craft foam.

Materials

- 5½"-tall glass fishbowl
- Darice Extra Thicky Foamies craft foam: orange
- Darice Foamies craft foam: black and green
- Coats Instant Stick & Hold for Crafts double-sided adhesive sheet
- Iridescent copper Scribbles 3-Dimensional Fabric Writer by Duncan Enterprises

Instructions

1. Following manufacturer's instructions, apply double-sided adhesive to backs of craft foam. Referring to patterns, cut shapes from craft foam.

2. Remove paper backing from foam pieces one piece at a time. Working in layers, apply the large pumpkin shape first, then the three smaller sections over it. Apply base of stem, then stem strips. Layer on orange pumpkin cheeks, and black eyes and mouth.

3. Lay bowl on table face up. Using iridescent copper paint, paint dots on stem strips and squiggles on cheeks; let dry. Let dry at least overnight before using. ***Note:** Fill with wrapped treats. Bowl can be wiped out with a damp cloth, but cannot be submerged in water.* ◆

—Design by Judi Kauffman

Felt Halloween Pins

Continued from page 121

ghost. Using 2 strands black floss, Backstitch "BOO" on front of ghost and sew mouth with Running Stitch.

3. Pin body pieces together; join with Blanket Stitch using 2 strands black embroidery floss and leaving opening for stuffing. Stuff body lightly with fiberfill and Blanket Stitch opening closed.

4. Sew or glue pin back to back of ghost.

Pumpkin

1. Referring to patterns (page 120), cut two pumpkins from pumpkin felt and one stem from kelly green felt.

2. On back of one pumpkin shape, sketch eyes and jack-o'-lantern mouth with fine-tip pen; cut out. Cut an oval of black felt large enough to cover eyes and mouth; glue lightly to wrong side of cutout pumpkin, making sure glue does not show through on front.

3. Pin pumpkins together, wrong sides facing. Join with Blanket Stitch using 2 strands black embroidery floss, catching end of stem between pumpkins at center top as you stitch and leaving opening for stuffing. Stuff body lightly with fiberfill and Blanket Stitch opening closed.

4. Cut two 6" x ⅛" strips from kelly green felt; wrap around knitting needle in spiral fashion, taping ends to hold securely. Sprinkle a little water on the felt strips. Place in a 250-degree oven for 15 minutes. Let cool completely before sliding felt coils off knitting needle. Fold spiral curls in half; tack centers to top of pumpkin with green embroidery floss, trimming ends as desired.

5. Sew or glue pin back to back of pumpkin. ◆

—Designs by Chris Malone

Watch Out for That Bat!

Just envision your Halloween party room with dozens of these bats dangling from the ceiling! Sound like fun? It is! Florist's wire lets you bend their wings in all kinds of high-flying shapes.

Materials

- ⅓ sheet black craft foam
- Black construction paper
- 2 (9") pieces florist's wire
- Clear adhesive package tape
- Craft glue
- 2 (15mm) red movable eyes
- Nylon thread, needle

Instructions

1. Referring to pattern, cut one bat from craft foam and one from construction paper.

2. Position wires 1" apart on one side of foam bat; tape down with package tape. Glue black paper bat to back of foam bat, sandwiching wires in between. Allow to dry completely.

3. Glue eyes to other foam side of bat.

4. Bend bat's wings as desired. Thread nylon thread through bat to hang as desired. ◆

—*Design by Mary T. Cosgrove*

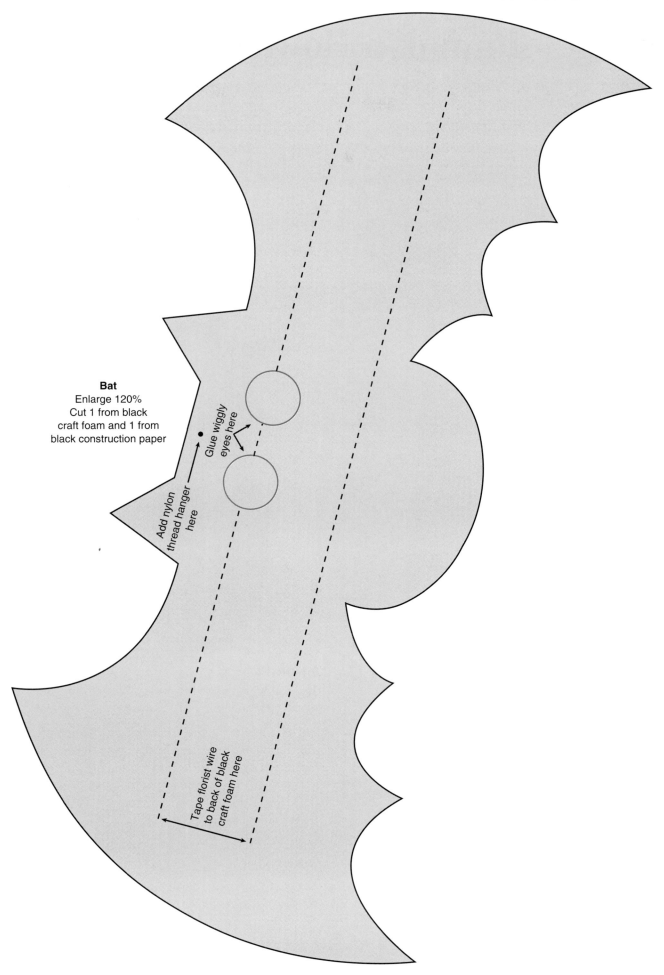

Bat
Enlarge 120%
Cut 1 from black
craft foam and 1 from
black construction paper

Glue wiggly
eyes here

Add nylon
thread hanger
here

Tape florist wire
to back of black
craft foam here

Pumpkin Bowling Pin

*Imagine a row of cheery characters like this one hanging from your country peg board …
or smiling faces hanging in your windows and adorning doorknobs throughout your home!
Precut bowling-pin shapes let you devote all your time to the fun part—painting!*

Materials

- 5½"-tall wooden bowling pin shape from Meadowood
- 1"-wide sponge brush
- Ceramcoat acrylic paints by Delta Technical Coatings:
  Pumpkin #02042
  Tangerine #02043
  Lavender #02047
  Straw #02078
  Lime green #02489
  White #02505
  Black #02506
  Brown iron oxide #02023
- Crackle medium by Delta Technical Coatings
- Antique brown #07301 stain by Delta Technical Coatings
- Glossy exterior varnish by Delta Technical Coatings
- Paintbrushes:
  #1 liner
  ½" flat glaze
  #8 flat shader
- Woodsies wooden shapes from Forster, Inc.:
  2 (1⅝") stars
  2 (1") triangles
  ⅜" circle
- Expandable sponge
- Craft glue
- 8" jute twine
- 10" orange Bedford Bendable Ribbon

Project Note

Comma strokes: Wet #1 liner brush; dry on paper towel; dip into paint. Press tip of brush down so that bristles of brush spread out, then slowly pull brush toward you and up onto tip of brush; lift off.

Instructions

1. Using ½" flat glaze brush, base-coat bowling-pin shape with tangerine.

2. Following instructions on crackle medium bottle, add crackle medium using #8 flat brush. When crackle medium is ready, refer to patterns and use #8 flat brush to base-coat stem with lime green. Use #8 shader to shade under stem with brown iron oxide and bottom of shape with pumpkin.

3. Using 1" sponge brush, give pumpkin a light coat of varnish; let dry.

4. Cut and moisten a small piece of expandable sponge. Squeeze out excess water; dip into antique brown.

Pumpkin Bowling Pin

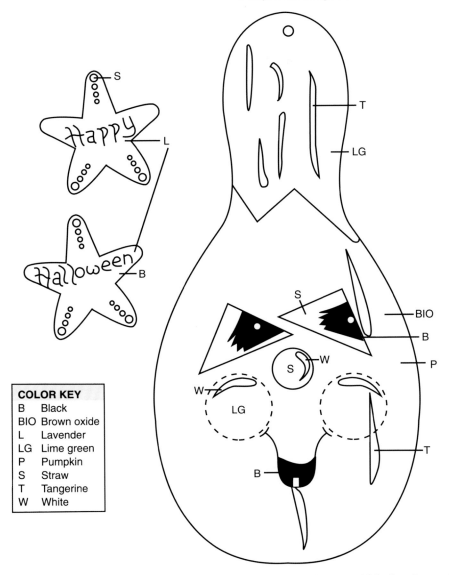

COLOR KEY
B	Black
BIO	Brown oxide
L	Lavender
LG	Lime green
P	Pumpkin
S	Straw
T	Tangerine
W	White

Sponge front of pumpkin until desired "cracks" appear. Set aside to dry.

5. Using ½" flat glaze brush, base-coat stars with lavender and circle and triangles with straw; let dry. Referring to photo and pattern, sponge cheeks onto pumpkin using lime green and a small piece of moistened expandable sponge. Paint mouth with black using #1 liner brush.

6. Glue eyes and nose to pumpkin using craft glue. Dip #1 liner brush into white and paint highlight dots on eyes; paint white comma strokes over tops of cheeks; paint in tooth.

7. Using #1 liner and black paint, paint "Happy" on one star and "Halloween" on the other. Place graduated dots of straw paint on stars as shown, using wooden handle end of #1 liner brush.

8. Coat completed pumpkin with varnish using 1" sponge brush.

9. Tie bendable ribbon around stem of pumpkin; coil ends around handle of #1 liner brush. Glue stars to end of each coil. Tie jute through top of pumpkin for hanging loop. ◆

—Design by Phyllis Sandford

A Day of Thanks

This Thanksgiving, take a moment to give thanks for the bounty of our land, and to remember the hard work it took our ancestors to settle it. As you celebrate this special holiday with family and friends, you'll want to add a variety of handsome and charming autumn crafts to your dinner table and home.

Bay Leaf Wreath & Mini Topiaries

Natural materials have always been part of elegant holiday decorations. Dried orange slices, star anise and filberts are just a few of the natural "ingredients" which make this festive wreath look good enough to eat! Or, think how nice your holiday table would look with a mini topiary at each place!

Materials

Bay Leaf Wreath

- 10" grapevine wreath
- Natural raffia
- Botanicals from Creative Chi:
  4 sprays preserved green cedar
  28 preserved bay leaves
  12 casurina pods
  10 dried rose hips
  12 star anise
  16 dried orange slices
  8 filberts (hazelnuts)
- Green paddle wire
- Low-temperature glue gun

Mini Topiaries

Makes 3 topiaries
- 3 (2½") plastic foam balls

- Botanicals from Creative Chi:
  1 cup blue juniper berries
  1 cup red juniper berries
  1 cup allspice berries
- 3 thin 3"-long cinnamon sticks
- 3 1¾"-diameter clay pots
- Floral clay
- Green moss
- Oakmoss
- Scraps of ⅛"-wide ribbon: ivory, red and silver
- Scraps of coordinating felt
- Ultra Gloss Metallic acrylic paints from DecoArt:
  True gold #DG37
  Bright gold #DG38
  Silver #DG39

  Bronze #DG40
- Americana acrylic paints from DecoArt:
  Snow white #DA1
  Blueberry #DA37
  Dark pine #DA49
  Teal green #DA107
  Santa red #DA170
  Alizarian crimson #DA179
- Small natural sponges
- #6 shader "cosmetic" artist's paintbrush #4300 from Loew-Cornell
- Low-temperature glue gun

Instructions

Bay Leaf Wreath

1. Referring to photo (page 128) throughout, glue preserved cedar to wreath, beginning at bottom and extending up over approximately two-thirds of both sides. Position and glue bay leaves around the wreath.

2. Tie raffia in 5"–6" bow; glue at top center of wreath. Glue one bay leaf, three casurina pods, two rose hips and one star anise to bow's center.

3. Cut four orange slices in half; glue whole and half slices around wreath. Add filberts and casurina pods. Fill in with star anise and rose hips.

—*Design by Creative Chi*

Mini Topiaries

Project Note

Consult general instructions for procedure; specific materials to be used for each of the three topiaries follow.

General Instructions

1. Coat plastic foam ball lightly with paint; let dry. Insert and glue cinnamon stick in base of ball for trunk.

2. Working on a small area at a time, spread glue on ball, then stick berries into glue to cover ball.

3. Paint pot with same color used on ball; let dry. Lightly sponge on second color; let dry. Very lightly sponge on third color; let dry. Go over pot one more time with an almost-dry sponge in topcoat color. Let dry. Add additional painted trim and details as desired.

4. Cut felt to fit bottom of pot; glue to bottom of pot.

5. Form a thick coil of floral clay to fit inside pot. Wrap coil around end of cinnamon stick and glue clay into pot. Holding topiary straight, allow glue to dry completely.

6. Glue bits of moss in top of pot to hide clay; tie ribbon in bow around cinnamon stick.

Continued on page 137

Turkey Pins

This clever design uses silk flower petals for the turkeys' multicolored tail feathers! Easy enough to make by the bunch, they'd also be delightful glued to simple felt loops for holiday napkin rings!

3. Take flower apart from center and base of flower. For each turkey, fold two flower layers in half; staple together. Hot-glue to back of body so petals form feathers.

4. Using dimensional paint and referring to pattern, dot on black eyes and add red wattle. Form beak by dotting on yellow paint and pulling up to form a point. Set aside to dry completely.

5. Place dots of adhesive on back of turkey. Following manufacturer's instructions, let dry for eight to 24 hours. Turkeys may then be adhered to place cards or napkin rings, or glued to pin back, and then used by your Thanksgiving guests. ▼

—Design by Janna Britton

Materials

- Felt in a variety of fall colors: tan, cranberry, cinnamon, etc.
- 4" silk chrysanthemum bloom in fall colors
- Scribbles Shiny Fabric Writers dimensional paints from Duncan Enterprises: bright yellow, black and red
- ⅛"-wide yellow-gold satin ribbon
- Stapler
- Aleene's Tack-It Over & Over adhesive
- Low-temperature glue gun
- Pin back

Instructions

1. Referring to pattern, cut turkey body from felt.

2. Cut 4½" piece ribbon for each turkey; tie knot ½" from each end. Fold ribbon in half; hot-glue ribbon to back of body at crease, letting knotted ends dangle for legs.

Turkey Pin
Cut 1 from felt for each pin

Turkey Gift Bag

*Tom's rainbow-bright tail transforms a brown paper bag into something special—
a lovely presentation for turkey-shaped cookies or other Thanksgiving treats!*

Materials

- 2 (4½" x 5½") sturdy brown paper gift bags, handles removed
- Craft foam sheets: red, brown, orange, black, yellow, light purple, royal blue, green, pink, light blue
- Pinking shears (optional)
- ¼" round paper punch
- White craft glue
- Black extra-fine-point marker
- 12" ¼"-wide red satin ribbon

Instructions

1. Referring to pattern, cut bag flap from extra paper bag; do not punch holes. Crease along fold line. Apply glue evenly to wrong side (inside) of small flap; press to backside of gift bag so larger flap covers gift bag opening and hangs down front. Let glue dry thoroughly, making sure excess glue does not seal bag shut.

2. Referring to patterns, cut turkey pieces from craft foam, cutting feathers with pinking shears if desired. Also, punch two circles from black craft foam for eyes.

3. Referring to photo throughout, mark detail lines on feathers with marker; glue feathers to wrong side of turkey body. Glue wings to front of body, and glue tops of feet to wrong sides of legs.

4. Crease foam heads along fold line so that one tab bends to the right and the other to the left. Sandwiching beak between heads, glue heads together up to creased lines; press tabs open and glue to body. Glue wattle to one side of turkey's head; glue eyes in place. Let glue dry completely.

5. Punch holes through all layers of bag and bag flap. Punch matching holes in turkey, positioning them so turkey will not extend below bottom of bag.

6. Glue turkey to front of bag flap, lining up holes; let dry.

7. Add treats to bag; fold turkey flap over front. Thread ribbon through holes in turkey and all layers of bag; tie in bow on front. ▼

—Design by Barbara A. Woolley

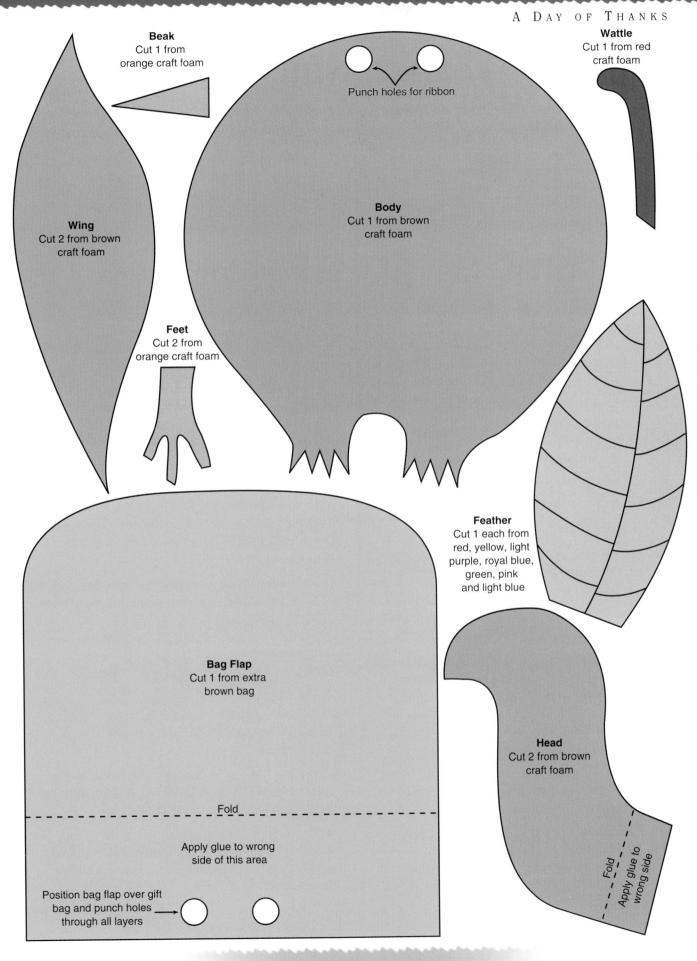

Beak
Cut 1 from
orange craft foam

Punch holes for ribbon

Wattle
Cut 1 from red
craft foam

Wing
Cut 2 from brown
craft foam

Body
Cut 1 from brown
craft foam

Feet
Cut 2 from
orange craft foam

Feather
Cut 1 each from
red, yellow, light
purple, royal blue,
green, pink
and light blue

Bag Flap
Cut 1 from extra
brown bag

Fold

Apply glue to wrong
side of this area

Head
Cut 2 from brown
craft foam

Fold

Apply glue to
wrong side

Position bag flap over gift
bag and punch holes
through all layers →

Thanksgiving Vest

Wear this beautiful vest to your family get-together and be prepared for rave reviews!
Only you will know how simple it was to craft this vest with all the look of a boutique original!

Materials

- Commercial vest pattern with no darts (see Project Note)
- 1½ yards main fabric for piecing, lining and binding
- 1 yard contrasting fabric
- Fabric scraps in assorted coordinating tan, rust and black prints, stripes, plaids and checks
- Scraps of green-and-rust print fabric for leaves
- Scraps of red prints for yo-yo berries
- Fusible webbing
- Coordinating sewing threads and monofilament
- Thin craft batting
- Assorted beads and/or small buttons
- 1½ yards narrow ribbon or braid for vine
- Tracing paper
- Chalk fabric-marking pencil

Project Note

Project was completed using McCall's pattern #7276.

Piecing & Embellishing

1. Referring to pattern, cut two fronts and one back for lining from main fabric, and one back for shell from main fabric. Cut two fronts from batting, cutting 1" larger all around. From each fabric except those for leaves and berries, cut two strips at least 18" long and 1¼", 1½" or 1¾" wide.

2. Stitch strips together into a sheet (see Fig. 1, page 136). Press all seam allowances in same direction. Cut 2½" slices from sheet (Fig. 2).

3. Referring to Fig. 3 and using chalk fabric pencil, draw borderline 3½" from edge of batting fronts. Place tracing paper over batting; trace borderline, adding ½" along inner edge (Fig. 4). Cut two borders from contrasting fabric, reversing one.

4. Place one pieced slice along center front borderline

(Fig. 5). Place second slice on first, right sides facing. Stitch along long edge; flip open (Fig. 6). Trim along borderline. Repeat until front panel (inside borderline) is covered (Fig. 7).

5. Place border panel on vest front with inner edge overlapping pieced panel ½". Turn edge under ¼" and pin in place. Stitch in place with narrow zigzag stitch using monofilament, or with a black or rust blanket stitch worked by hand or machine.

6. Referring to pattern for berries (page 136), cut at least 18 berries from red prints.

7. Turn under ⅛" all around on fabric circles; stitching by hand and using coordinating thread, sew gathering stitch along fold. Pull gathering thread tight; knot. Press flat to form yo-yo.

8. Bond fusible webbing to wrong side of leaf fabrics; referring to pattern, cut out at least 12 leaves.

9. Draw a meandering line on right side of one vest front (Fig. 8). Place ribbon or narrow braid along line. Couch in place with a blind hem stitch or zigzag using monofilament thread.

10. Arrange half of leaves along vine; fuse. Stitch around each leaf by hand using blanket stitch and black thread.

11. Repeat steps 9 and 10 on remaining vest front.

Construction

1. Press vest fronts with steam iron. Place paper pattern on vest fronts; cut to size.

2. Using ⅝" seam allowance through step 3, stitch lining together along shoulder and side seams. Press seams open.

3. Stitch vest pieces together along shoulder and side seams; press seams open. Whenever possible, trim batting out of seam allowances to reduce bulk.

4. Pin vest and lining together, wrong sides facing and matching shoulder seams and points. Stitch around vest armholes and periphery using ¾" seam allowance. Trim seam allowance to ¼".

5. Using monofilament, stitch in the ditch through vest and lining from the outside along seam.

Binding

1. Cut 18" square from binding fabric. Cut diagonally to create triangles (Fig. 9).

2. Set stitch length on sewing machine to 12–14 stitches per inch. Sew two triangles together, right sides facing (Fig. 10). Press seam open.

3. Mark lines every 2½" on wrong side of fabric (Fig. 11).

4. Bring short ends together, right sides facing, offsetting one line (Fig. 12), and stitch.

The piece will now be a tube (it will feel awkward). Press seam open.

5. Begin cutting at point A and follow cutting lines in a spiral fashion until all bias is cut in one continuous strip.

6. Fold binding in half lengthwise, wrong sides facing; press with iron.

7. Position raw edges of binding along raw edge of vest on right side; pin. Stitch using ½" seam allowance.

8. Fold binding to vest inside, encasing raw edges. Using monofilament thread, stitch in place by hand or machine.

9. Bind armholes in a similar manner, making additional binding (steps 1–6) as needed.

10. Position yo-yo "berries" in clusters along ribbon or braid vine; hand-stitch using coordinating thread. Stitch a bead (or beads) in the center of each yo-yo. ▼

—*Design by Beth Wheeler*

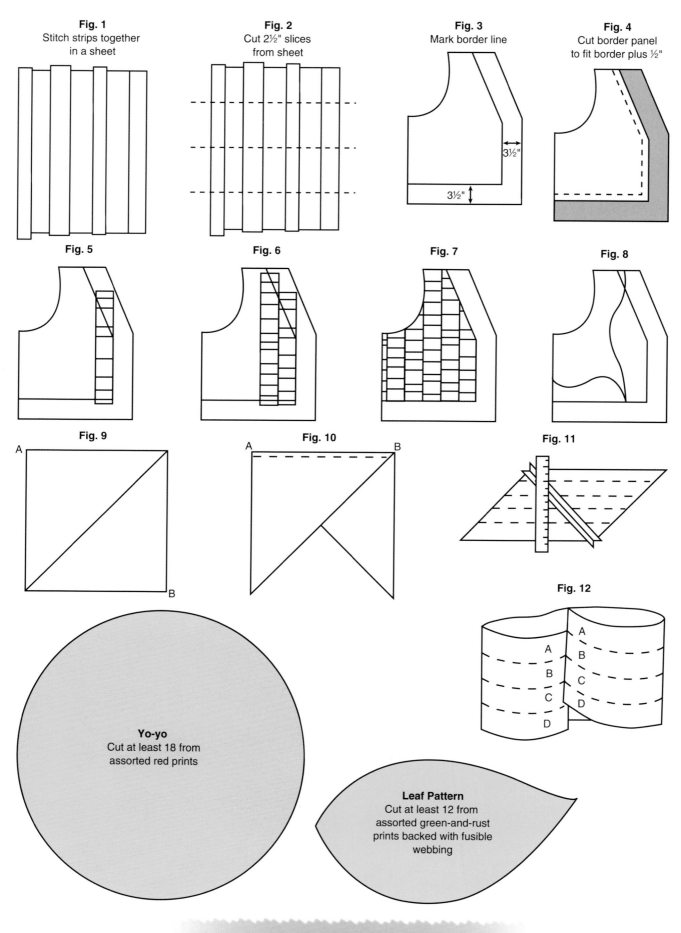

Fig. 1
Stitch strips together
in a sheet

Fig. 2
Cut 2½" slices
from sheet

Fig. 3
Mark border line

3½"

3½"

Fig. 4
Cut border panel
to fit border plus ½"

Fig. 5

Fig. 6

Fig. 7

Fig. 8

Fig. 9

A

B

Fig. 10

A   B

Fig. 11

Fig. 12

A
A
B
B
C
C
D
D

Yo-yo
Cut at least 18 from
assorted red prints

Leaf Pattern
Cut at least 12 from
assorted green-and-rust
prints backed with fusible
webbing

Harvest Pumpkin

Stitch a remarkably lifelike pumpkin from plastic canvas!

Materials

- 1 sheet Darice Super Soft 7-count plastic canvas
- #16 tapestry needle
- Uniek Needloft plastic canvas yarn as listed in color key
- Hot-glue gun

Instructions

1. Cut plastic canvas as indicated on graphs.

2. Stitch pieces as shown, reversing one stem piece.

3. Using mint, Overcast edges of leaf; using avocado, Whipstitch stem halves together.

4. Using pumpkin yarn through step 5, Whipstitch two pumpkin sections together along inner curve, right sides of stitched pieces facing. Repeat with remaining sections to form 12 joined sections.

5. Whipstitch one joined section to another along outer curve with wrong sides of stitched pieces facing. Repeat with remaining sections until all are joined in one piece; Whipstitch remaining edges together to form round pumpkin.

6. Hot-glue stem in hole at top of pumpkin; hot-glue leaf in place. ▼

—Design by Angie Arickx

COLOR KEY	
Plastic Canvas Yarn	**Yards**
▨ Pumpkin #12	45
▨ Mint #24	3
▨ Avocado #30	2
Color numbers given are for Uniek Needloft plastic canvas yarn.	

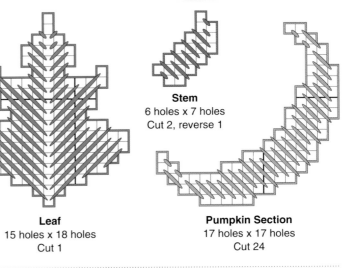

Stem
6 holes x 7 holes
Cut 2, reverse 1

Leaf
15 holes x 18 holes
Cut 1

Pumpkin Section
17 holes x 17 holes
Cut 24

Mini Topiaries

Continued from page 130

Blue Juniper Topiary

Paint ball and pot with dark pine; add second coat with silver, third coat with blueberry and topcoat with teal green. Use oakmoss and silver ribbon.

Red Juniper Topiary

Paint ball and pot with alizarian crimson; add second coat with Santa red, third coat with white and topcoat with alizarian crimson. Use green moss and red ribbon.

Allspice Topiary

Paint ball and pot with bronze; add second coat with bright gold, third coat with true gold and topcoat with white. Use green moss and ivory ribbon. ▼

—Designs by Creative Chi

Happy Harvest

Tradition tells us that Indians and Pilgrims shared their bounty on the very first Thanksgiving. Commemorate that first festive event with this colorful magnet.

Materials

- Polyform Sculpey III modeling compound:

  Green #022

  Orange #032

  Black #042

  Brown #052

  Chocolate #053

  Yellow #072

  Red #082

  Flesh #092

  Tan #301
- 4 black seed beads
- Straight-edge tool for
- cutting and making lines
- Round toothpick
- ½" round magnet
- Craft glue
- Small white feather

Pilgrim

1. Cut off ¼ section of flesh modeling compound; cut this small piece in half, then cut one of the halves in half again, giving you ¼ of the original ¼ section. Soften compound between your fingers and roll into a ball. Flatten ball and shape it into a ¼"-thick circle.

2. Referring to photo throughout, press two black seed beads on their sides into head for eyes; press just until none of the bead hole shows.

3. Rub red modeling compound with your little finger; transfer color onto face for cheeks.

4. Roll a tiny ball of flesh compound for nose; press gently onto face.

5. For hair, soften a ball of yellow compound half the size of a marble; form into an even rope by rolling it back and forth on the work surface with your palm. Flatten this rope and cut into about seven ½"-long strands. Attach three for bangs and two on each side for hair, trimming as necessary.

Hat

1. Cut off ¼ section of chocolate modeling compound; cut this small piece in half, then cut one of the halves in half again. Cut this small piece in half one more time to give you ⅛ of the original ¼ section. Soften com-pound between your fingers and roll into a ball.

2. Squeeze center of ball slightly, then pinch sides so bottom is wider than top. Flatten top on work surface to give it square look. Flatten bottom on table and make hat brim by forming a ridge all around the hat; flatten top of hat again as needed.

3. Roll a ball of brown compound half the size of a pea into a small, even rope. Flatten into hatband; attach around hat with ends meeting in back; trim any excess. Press hat gently onto Pilgrim's head.

Pilgrim's Arms

1. Soften and roll a marble-size ball of chocolate com-pound; cut in half. Roll each half into 1"-long arm; attach a ball of flesh compound half the size of a pea at one end of each arm for hands.

2. Attach right arm to base of Pilgrim's head; set other arm aside for now.

Pumpkin

1. Cut off ¼ section of orange modeling compound; cut this small piece in half, then cut one of the halves in half again, giving you ¼ of the original ¼ section. Soften compound between your fingers and roll into a ball. Flatten ball and shape it into a ⅞"-wide circle.

2. Using round toothpick, poke hole in top to accept stem. Using smooth straight edge, incise lines on pumpkin, working from top of pumpkin to bottom.

3. For stem, soften and roll a ball of green compound half the size of a pea. Shape into a cone and insert point into hole in pumpkin. Place pumpkin in Pilgrim's right arm.

Indian

1. Repeat steps 1–4 of Pilgrim, substituting tan compound for flesh.

2. For hair, soften and roll a ball of black compound the size of a marble. Cut in half; roll and shape each half into a teardrop shape, continuing to elongate and flatten the pointed ends for braids; twist to resemble braids. Attach wide ends of pieces to top of head so wide ends meet in center of head.

3. Twist a small rope of red compound for headband; wrap around head with ends meeting in back; trim any excess.

Indian's Arms

1. Soften and roll a ball of tan compound the size of a marble; cut in half and roll each into a 1"-long arm, flattening and rounding end of each for hand.

2. Attach left arm to base of Indian's head; set other arm aside for now.

Corn

1. Roll two pea-size balls of yellow compound. Form each into a ¾"-long ear of corn, rounding ends. Using smooth straight edge, incise vertical and horizontal lines to simulate kernels.

2. For leaves, roll four pea-size balls of green compound. Flatten and form each into 1"-long teardrop shape. Attach rounded end at bottom of corn, bringing leaf up side and curling tip of leaf slightly. Repeat with remaining leaves, attaching two to each ear of corn. Carefully position ears of corn in crook of Indian's arm; press pumpkin and corn together firmly.

Arms

1. Attach Pilgrim's remaining arm back around Indian; hand should be on Indian's shoulder and other end should be attached under Pilgrim's head.

2. Flatten Indian's remaining arm a bit and attach hand first on Pilgrim's shoulder; trim off any excess arm.

Finishing

1. Transfer molded figure to an oven-proof plate. Bake in a preheated 275-degree oven for 10 minutes; cool completely.

2. Glue magnet to back of figure.

3. Cut tip from feather and glue to back of Indian's head, trimming as needed. ▼

—Design by Jackie Haskell

Autumn Glory Greeting Card

Here's a clever idea for beautiful invitations or note cards. A packet of half a dozen of these quick and easy cards tied up with some seasonal ribbon would make a lovely hostess gift!

Instructions

1. Following manufacturer's instructions, fuse webbing to wrong sides of fabrics and ribbon. Referring to photo throughout, cut three leaf shapes from fabric.

Materials
- 5" x 7" blank card stock
- Fusible webbing
- Fabric scraps in leaf prints or other autumn designs
- 6" 1½"-wide coordinating ribbon
- Metallic gold marking pen

2. Position leaves on front of card; fuse to card front. Position ribbon diagonally over corner; fuse. Let cool; trim excess ribbon.

3. Using metallic gold pen, outline leaves with a dashed line. ▼

—Design by Blanche Lind

Happy Hanukkah

Make your family's Hanukkah celebration one to be cherished for years to come by including a fun tic-tac-toe game the kids will love, a beautiful table runner and Star of David cards to share with loved ones.

Hanukkah Table Runner

This striking table topper in blue and metallic gold is easy to stitch up in a hurry.

Materials

- 1 yard blue-and-gold print fabric
- ¾ yard metallic gold brocade fabric
- 1 yard fusible lightweight interfacing
- 1 yard Wonder-Under fusible web from Pellon
- ½ yard craft fleece
- 1 spool metallic gold thread
- 1 spool gold sewing thread
- Sewing machine with open-toe and walking feet
- Iron and pressing cloth

Instructions

1. Fuse interfacing to wrong side of brocade fabric using a pressing cloth.

2. Referring to patterns, draw all pattern pieces on smooth side of fusible web; fuse marked web to back of brocade fabric using pressing cloth. Cut out all pieces.

3. From print fabric, cut two pieces each 18" x 40½". From craft fleece, cut one piece 18" x 40½". From gold brocade, cut two binding strips 1½" x 41" and two binding strips 1½" x 18½".

4. Referring to photo (page 140) for placement, position gold brocade cutouts on right side of one of the blue-and-gold print panels. Peel off backing; fuse cutouts in place using pressing cloth.

5. Thread machine with metallic gold thread; thread bobbin with gold sewing thread. Set machine for a medium-wide, slightly open zigzag stitch. Using open-toe foot, machine-appliqué around each cutout.

6. Place remaining panel of blue-and-gold print (backing) facedown on work surface; lay fleece on wrong side of backing and top on fleece, right side up. Center top of runner; smooth out. Pin or baste layers together at regular intervals.

7. Set machine for wider stitch than you used to appliqué cutouts. Machine-appliqué around each cutout again, stitching over first layer of stitching and attaching all three layers.

8. Replace open-toe foot with walking foot. Set machine for long straight stitch.

Star of David
Cut 1 on fold
from gold

Fold

Machine-quilt over background and cutouts in long, wavy lines, starting at one end and reversing at the other end, going back and forth until entire runner is machine-quilted.

9. Trim edges of runner even; machine-quilt along edges.

10. Place long brocade strips on top of runner along long edges, right sides facing. Stitch ¼" from edges. Fold binding strips over to wrong side of runner; turn under raw edges and stitch by hand. Repeat with short strips along short edges, folding in edges at corners. Trim all loose threads. ✡

—Design by Charlyne Stewart

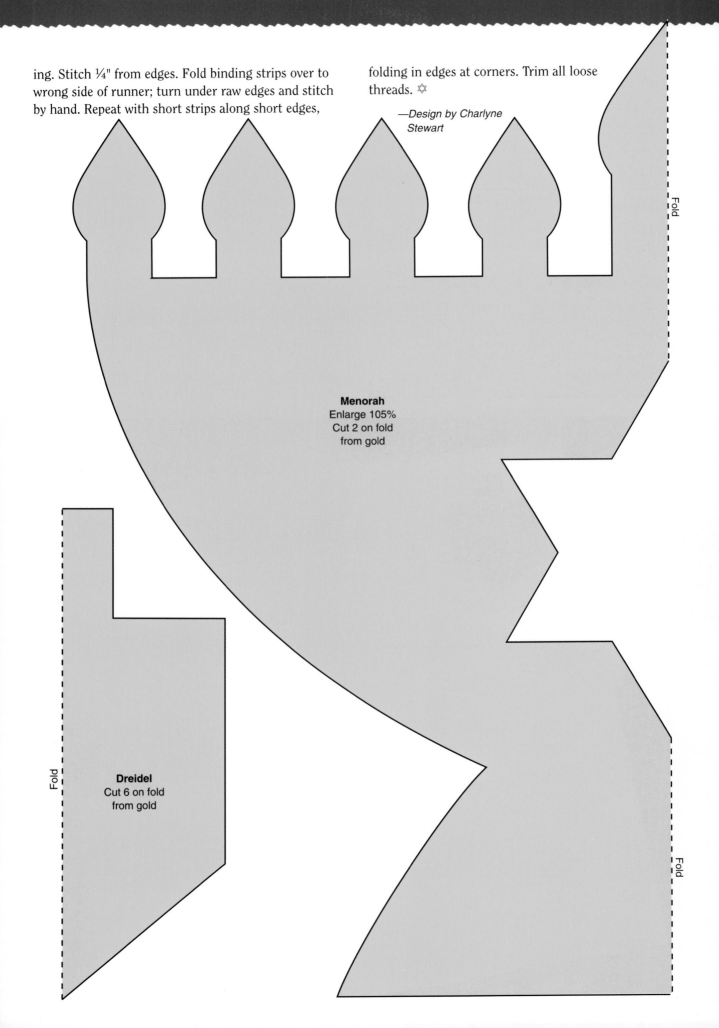

Menorah
Enlarge 105%
Cut 2 on fold
from gold

Dreidel
Cut 6 on fold
from gold

Fold

Fold

Fold

Hanukkah Tic-Tac-Toe

*Colorful dreidels and Hanukkah candles are the playing
pieces for this fun version of a childhood classic.*

Materials

- Craft foam:

  9" square white

  Small pieces of blue,
  green, orange, dark pink,
  navy blue and yellow

- Black permanent fine-tip
  marking pen

- Wright's metallic gold #046 rickrack

- Tacky craft glue

Instructions

1. Referring to patterns, cut four dreidels—one each
from blue, green, orange and dark pink craft foam. Cut
Hebrew letters from navy blue craft foam. Cut four candles from yellow and four flames from orange. Also cut
½" spacer squares to fit on backs of playing pieces—four
yellow, and one each blue, green, orange and dark pink.

2. Referring to patterns, draw outline around each dreidel, candle and flame using black fine-tip marking pen.

3. Glue Hebrew letter to right side of each dreidel; glue
spacer square of matching color to back of each dreidel.

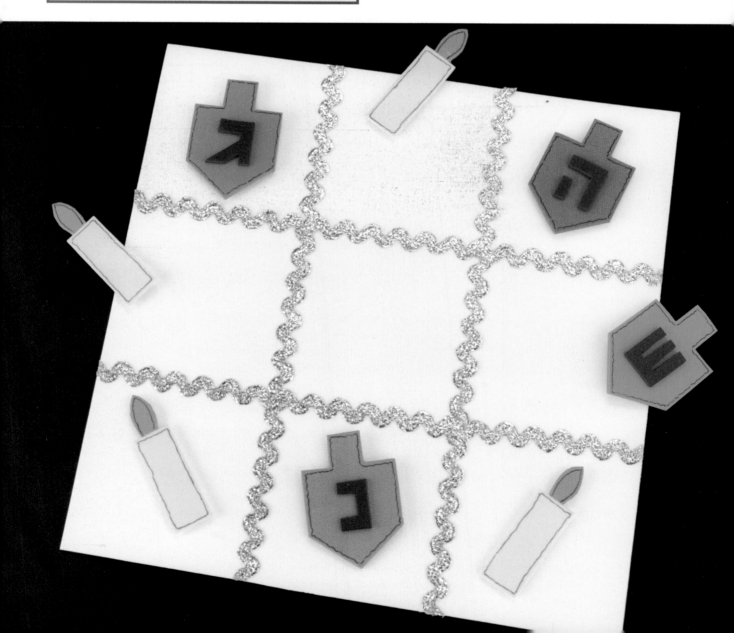

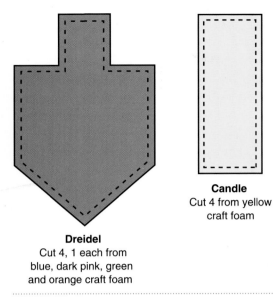

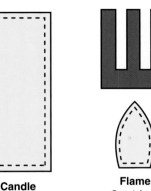

Hebrew Letters
Cut 1 of each letter
from navy craft foam

Dreidel
Cut 4, 1 each from
blue, dark pink, green
and orange craft foam

Candle
Cut 4 from yellow
craft foam

Flame
Cut 4 from
orange craft foam

4. Glue candle flame atop each candle, attaching edge to edge. Glue yellow spacer square to back of each candle.

5. Cut four 9" strips of gold rickrack. Glue to white craft foam to make game board. Let all pieces dry thoroughly. ✡

—*Design by Helen L. Rafson*

Star of David Card

Send heartfelt Hanukkah greetings to those you love with this beautiful handmade card.

Materials

- Strathmore 5" x 6⅞" blank greeting card #105-150 or 105-120
- 6 Woodsies medium wooden diamonds from Forster Inc.
- FolkArt acrylic paints from Plaid Enterprises, Inc.:
  Ivory white #427
  Sterling blue #441
  Baby blue #442
- Fine-point black permanent marking pen
- Matte-finish varnish
- Tacky craft glue
- Waxed paper

Instructions

1. Add a few drops of water to a small puddle of ivory white paint. Referring to photo throughout, paint half of each diamond white. Let paint dry.

2. Add a few drops of water to a small puddle of sterling blue paint; paint other half of each diamond with sterling blue. Paint edges also. Let paint dry.

3. Decorate sterling blue portions of diamonds with tiny baby blue dots; let dry.

4. Brush painted diamonds with matte varnish; let dry.

5. Using black marking pen, draw 4" square in center of card, drawing in a "running stitch." Glue diamonds in star shape.

6. Cover card with a piece of waxed paper; press flat under heavy books. When flat, outline star with "running stitch," using fine-point marker; also add running stitch between white and blue on each diamond. ✡

—*Design by Kathy Wegner*

A Merry Christmas

Deck the halls, trim the tree and give gifts galore during this most festive of holidays! This collection of Christmas crafts will meet many of your holiday needs, from pretty decorations to the perfect gift for that special someone. These crafts are so cute and so much fun to make that you'll find yourself working on them all throughout the year!

Reindeer Sweatshirt

This cuddly sweatshirt with its colorful design is perfect for leisure wear throughout the holidays! See photo on previous page

Materials

- Adult black sweatshirt
- Felt: green, gold, red, cashmere tan, white and black
- 9" square tan Rainbow Shaggy Plush Felt by Kunin Felt
- ⅛ yard Pellon Fusible Fleece
- ½ yard Pellon Heavy-Duty Wonder-Under transfer web
- 2 (⅛") black buttons
- ½" red button
- Black 6-strand embroidery floss
- Sewing thread: red and black

Instructions

1. Prewash sweatshirt without using fabric softener.

2. Following manufacturer's instructions, apply fusible fleece to back of red felt; apply transfer web to back of all felt. Referring to patterns (also see page 150), cut pieces from felt and plush felt as indicated. Remove paper backing.

3. Referring to photo and placement diagram (page 150), position pieces on sweatshirt. Place pressing cloth over design area; fuse in place.

4. Using 2 strands black embroidery floss, Blanket Stitch around all appliqués.

5. Sew a black button to each bird for eye; sew red button to holly for berry. ✳

—Design by Angie Wilhite

Project Note

Refer to photo throughout for placement.

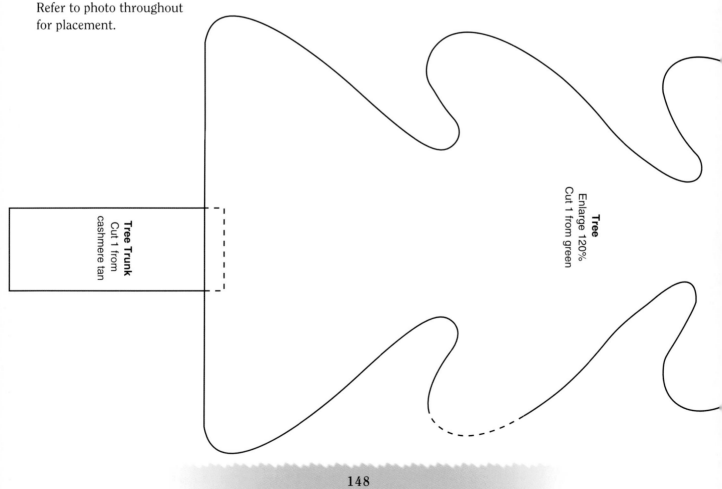

Tree Trunk
Cut 1 from cashmere tan

Tree
Enlarge 120%
Cut 1 from green

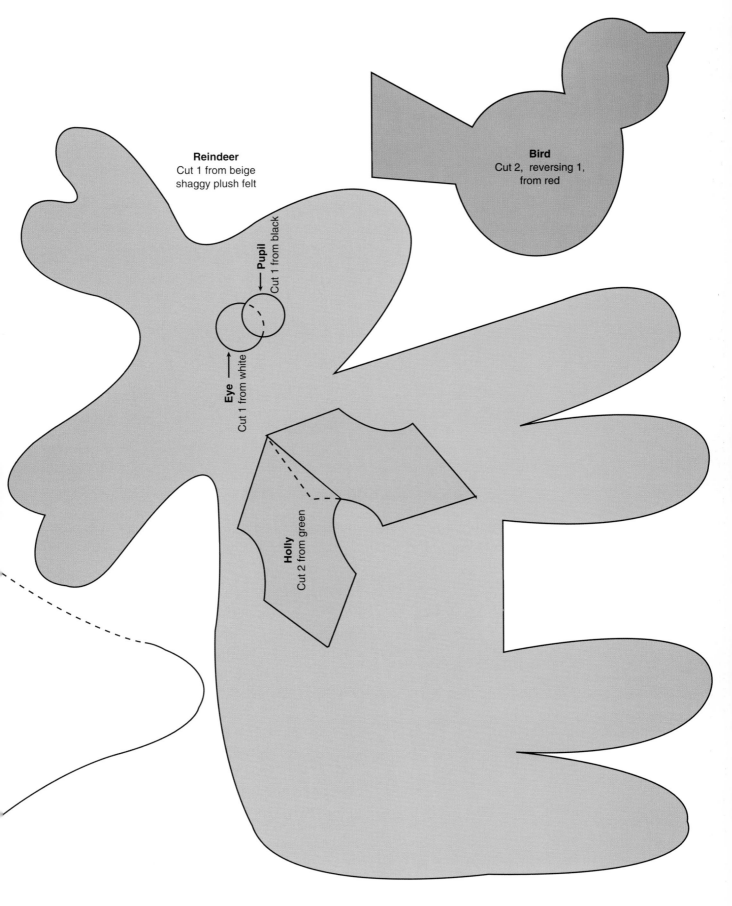

Reindeer
Cut 1 from beige
shaggy plush felt

Bird
Cut 2, reversing 1,
from red

Pupil
Cut 1 from black

Eye
Cut 1 from white

Holly
Cut 2 from green

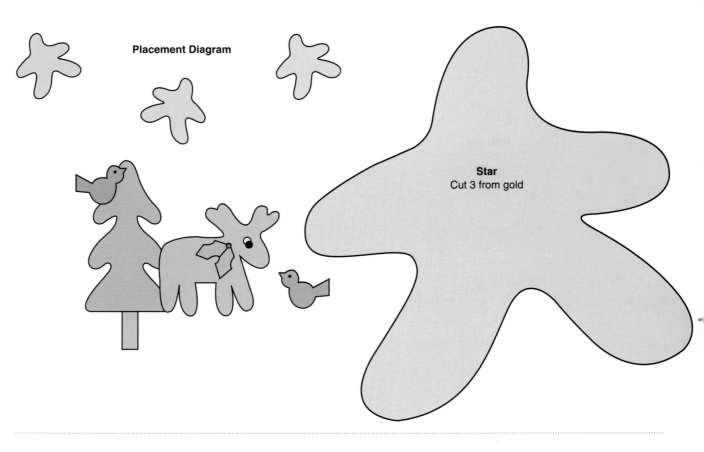

Placement Diagram

Star
Cut 3 from gold

Reindeer Vest

*Be prepared for compliments when you wear this colorful, cheerful vest
with its friendly reindeer motif. Great gift idea, too! See photo on page 146.*

Materials
- Adult antique white Classic Rainbow Felt Vest by Kunin Felt
- 12" square brown sugar Rainbow Shaggy Plush Felt by Kunin Felt
- Felt: antique gold, denim, sage, black, cranberry and cinnamon
- ½ yard Pellon Heavy-Duty Wonder-Under transfer web
- DMC 6-strand embroidery floss:
  Black #310
  Gold #729
- Black thread
- 5 (⅛") black buttons

Project Note
Refer to photo throughout for placement.

Instructions
1. Following manufacturer's instructions, apply transfer web to back of all felt. Referring to patterns (also see pages 152 and 153), cut pieces from felt and plush felt as indicated. Remove paper backing.

2. Referring to photo and placement diagram (page 153) position pieces on vest fronts. Place pressing cloth over design area; fuse in place.

3. Using 3 strands black embroidery floss, Blanket Stitch around armholes and edges of vest, and around moon, antlers, birds, reindeer head, body, arms, legs and tree trunks. Backstitch reindeer's mouth.

4. Using 3 strands gold embroidery floss, Blanket Stitch around stars, trees, nose and hooves.

Continued on page 153

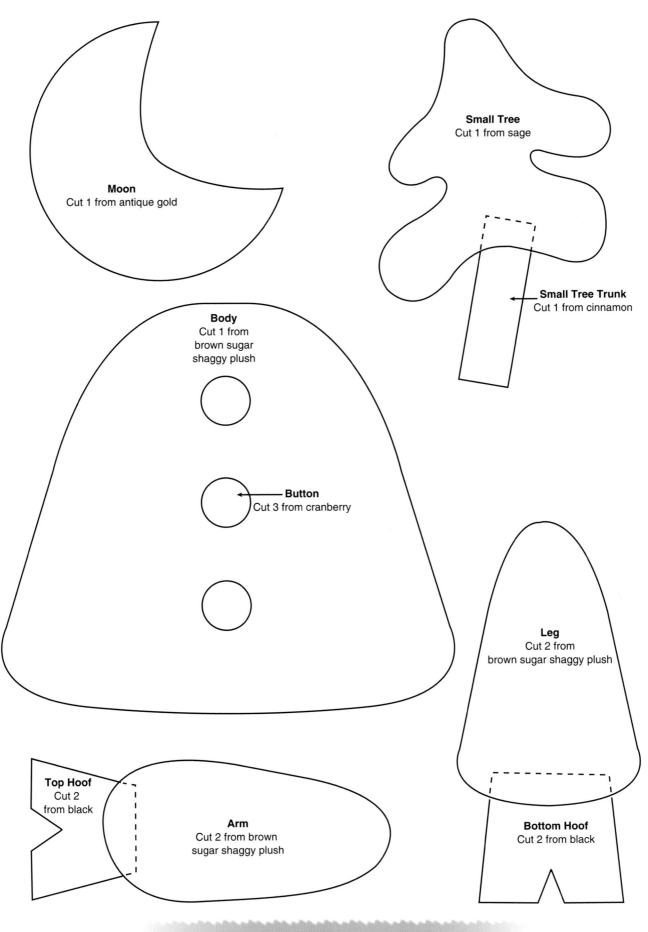

Moon
Cut 1 from antique gold

Small Tree
Cut 1 from sage

Small Tree Trunk
Cut 1 from cinnamon

Body
Cut 1 from
brown sugar
shaggy plush

Button
Cut 3 from cranberry

Leg
Cut 2 from
brown sugar shaggy plush

Top Hoof
Cut 2
from black

Arm
Cut 2 from brown
sugar shaggy plush

Bottom Hoof
Cut 2 from black

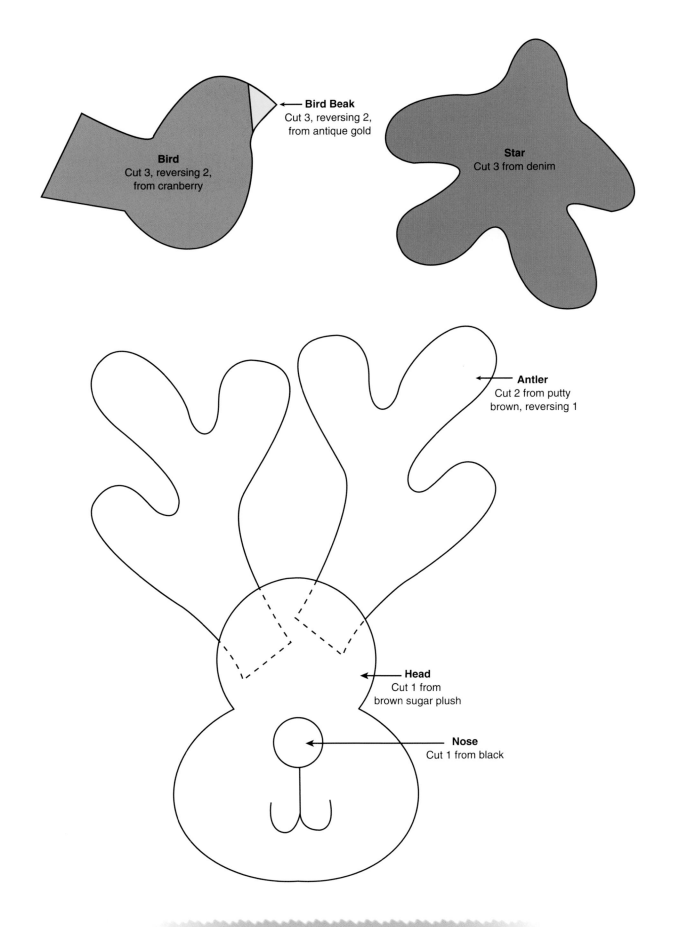

Bird Beak
Cut 3, reversing 2,
from antique gold

Bird
Cut 3, reversing 2,
from cranberry

Star
Cut 3 from denim

Antler
Cut 2 from putty
brown, reversing 1

Head
Cut 1 from
brown sugar plush

Nose
Cut 1 from black

Placement Diagram

Continued from page 150

5. Using 2 strands black embroidery floss, sew a single stitch in the center of each cranberry button to attach.

6. Using black sewing thread, sew button eyes to birds and reindeer. ✳

—*Design by Angie Wilhite*

Large Tree
Cut 1 from sage

Large Tree Trunk
Cut 1 from cinnamon

Wire Hanger Angel

Invite this sweet little cherub with corkscrew curls and a country halo to share your holidays!

Materials
- 5" x 8" x ½" wood
- Scroll saw or band saw
- Drill
- Paintbrushes
- Fine-grit sandpaper
- Wood sealer
- FolkArt acrylic paints from Plaid Enterprises, Inc.:
  Ivory white #427
  Terra cotta #433
  Lipstick red #437
  Leaf green #447
  Green forest #448
  Parchment #450
  Cappuccino #451
  Cinnamon #913
  Skintone #949
- Apple Barrel acrylic paint from Plaid Enterprises, Inc.:
  Country tan #20778
- Black fine-point permanent marking pen
- 10" 19-gauge black wire
- Hot-glue gun or all-purpose craft glue
- Matte varnish: brush-on or aerosol

Instructions

1. Referring to pattern, cut out angel shape. Drill hole ½" deep into top center edge. Sand. Coat with sealer; let dry. Sand again.

2. Transfer pattern markings to wood as needed. Base-coat face and hands with skintone; shade around hair-line and neckline with cinnamon. Dry-brush cheeks with cinnamon.

3. Base-coat wings with parchment; shade with country tan. Float inner wing area with ivory white.

4. Base-coat hair with cappuccino; shade with terra cotta.

5. Base-coat dress with leaf green; shade with green forest.

6. Base-coat ruffle with lipstick red; float highlight along very edge with ivory white.

7. Using lipstick red, paint hearts on dress.

8. When all paints are thoroughly dry, outline and add details with black marking pen.

9. Referring to Figs. 1–3, bend wire into hanger; glue ends in hole drilled in top of angel.

10. Draw with marking pen on scrap of wood and coat with varnish; if ink runs when brush-on varnish is applied, use aerosol varnish. Apply two coats varnish; let dry completely. ❊

—*Design by Kathy Wegner*

Fig. 1

Fig. 2

Fig. 3

1¼"→

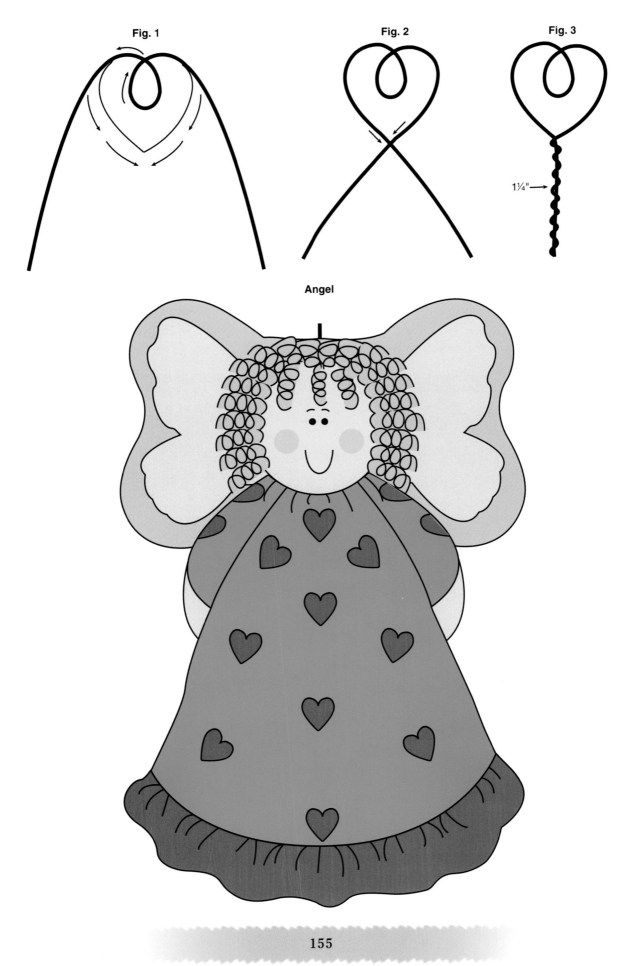

Angel

Painted Paper Santas

*These cuties work up in a hurry! Their "beards" are
ready-made doilies—what fun for tree and package trims!*

Materials

- 4" x 8" brown heavy-weight paper
- 4" square Pellon Wonder-Under transfer web
- 4" square Pellon fusible fleece
- 3" square Pellon Heavy-Duty Wonder-Under transfer web
- 3" square muslin fabric
- 2½"-wide white crocheted doily #MC ASST from Wimpole

Street Creations
- Acrylic paints: bright red and black
- 2 Woodsies medium wooden hearts from Forster Inc.
- 9" ⅛"-wide red satin ribbon
- 4" ¼"-wide red satin ribbon
- 5mm red pompon
- Camel sewing thread
- 2 (7mm) black movable eyes

- Crafty Magic Melt Floral Pro low-temperature glue gun with needle nozzle and Crafty Magic Melt jewelry-glue sticks from Adhesive Technologies, Inc.

Continued on page 163

Joyful Bear

Craft this angelic teddy from modeling compound, then hang him from the tree or use him to decorate your gift packages!

Materials
- Polyform Sculpey III modeling compound:
  Green #022
  Black #042
  Yellow #072
  Red #082
  Tan #301
  Ivory #501
- 2 black seed beads
- Straight-edge tool for cutting and making lines
- Straight pin
- Paintbrush with wooden handle
- 24-gauge wire
- All-purpose glitter spray
- Cardboard

Body

1. Cut off ¼ section of tan modeling compound; cut this small piece in half, then cut one of the halves in half again, giving you ¼ of the original ¼ section. Soften compound between your fingers and roll into a ball.

2. Shape the ball on the work surface into a teardrop shape; the back should remain flat. With thumb and forefinger, pinch sides of the rounded end; this is where legs will be attached.

Arms

1. Roll two pea-size balls from tan modeling compound. Roll each on the work surface until it is a ¾"-long cone shape; make the two arms as identical as possible.

2. Flatten and shape the thicker end of both cones to make paws. Attach arms at top of body.

Head

1. Cut off ¼ section of tan modeling compound; cut this small piece in half. Soften and roll this piece into a ball. Set ball on work surface; referring to photo and Fig. 1 throughout, form ball into a

Fig. 1

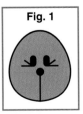

squat teardrop shape, keeping the back of the head flat on the table.

2. Press two black seed beads on their sides into head for eyes; press just until none of the bead hole shows.

3. Rub red modeling compound with your little finger; transfer color onto face for cheeks.

4. Using smooth straight edge, make a vertical line separating the cheeks, starting below the eyes and ending at the bottom of the head. Using straight pin, mark eyelashes at corners of eyes.

5. Roll a tiny ball of black compound for nose; press gently onto face at top of slit. Gently press head onto body.

6. For ears, roll pea-size ball of tan compound; cut in half. Flatten slightly. With end of wooden paintbrush handle, indent ear; keeping ear on tip of paintbrush handle, place on head, attaching it firmly. Repeat with other ear.

Legs

1. Roll a ball of tan modeling compound the size of a marble; cut in half. Soften and roll each half into a ¾"-long log.

Continued on page 170

Foam Reindeer Ornament

A few pieces of craft foam make a wonderful ornament for tree, packages or lapel!

Materials

- Craft foam:
  2" x 2½" brown
  2¼" tan square
  3" square green
  Scraps red and white
- 8¼" string mini imitation tree lights
- Low-temperature glue gun or tacky craft glue
- Fine-point brown marking pen
- ¼" round paper punch
- String for hanging loop, self-adhesive magnet strip or 1" pin back

Instructions

1. Referring to patterns, cut head, antlers and wreath as directed. Using hole punch, punch two circles from white for eyes, and one red circle for nose.

2. Referring to Fig. 1 and photo, position string of lights on wreath; glue antlers over top of lights. Glue head over antlers.

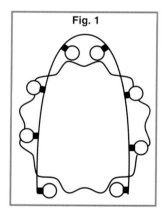

Fig. 1

3. Glue on eyes and nose. Using brown marking pen, ink in pupils on eyes; add eyebrows and lines along edges of ears.

4. Finish as desired with string for hanging, magnet strip or pin back. ✳

—Design by Kathy Wegner

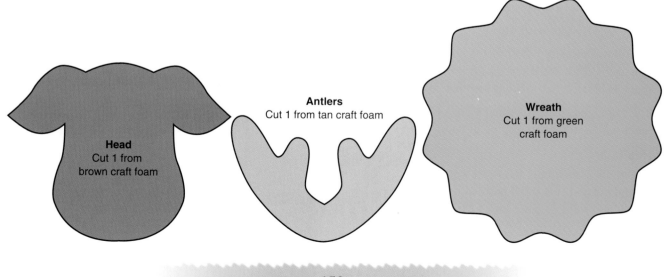

Head
Cut 1 from brown craft foam

Antlers
Cut 1 from tan craft foam

Wreath
Cut 1 from green craft foam

Ribbon Angel

*Make these angels in a variety of holiday ribbons to tie to packages, greenery
and your tree—or glue on a pin back and wear one on your lapel!*

Materials

- 1" gold ball ornament
- 14" 2"–2½"-wide wire-edge holiday ribbon with gold highlights
- 3½" wired gold cord
- 12" ⅝"-wide wire-edged gold ribbon
- 8" gold cord
- Large-eye hand-sewing needle and coordinating thread
- Low temperature glue gun

Instructions

1. Remove wire end from gold ball ornament; discard.

2. Cut holiday ribbon into one 8" piece for wings and one 6" piece for body.

3. Fold down cut edges of 6" piece of ribbon ¼"; using coordinating sewing thread, run gathering stitches across one end and into opposite end, pulling ends together to make a circle. Before closing circle, apply glue to stem of ornament and insert stem into gathers. Pull thread tight; close circle and knot.

4. Referring to photo throughout, form wired gold cord into a circle for halo; glue to back of head.

5. For wings, find center of 8" piece of ribbon; fold both ends so they overlap ¼" at center. Sew gathering stitch along center through all three layers. Pull up gathers tightly and wrap thread several times around center; knot thread and clip. Glue wings to back of head.

6. Tie wire-edged gold ribbon into bow. Glue to front of angel below head. Arrange ribbon tails as desired; trim ends at an angle.

7. Thread gold cord into needle and run through top of wings. Knot ends and clip. ✳

—Design by Chris Malone

Stacked Christmas Keepsake Boxes

These pretty boxes are as functional as they are decorative! Use them to stash spare fuses for the tree lights, or ornament hooks, or gift tags, or cocktail napkins … or gifts!

Materials

- Set of 3 nesting oval papier-mâché picture-frame boxes
- ¼ yard fabric with Christmas motifs from Leslie Beck for V.I.P.
- ½ yard coordinating checked holiday fabric from Leslie Beck for V.I.P.
- ½ yard coordinating burgundy fabric
- Scrap fabrics
- 1½ yards ⅜"–½"-wide gold-and-burgundy trim
- Holiday Assortment crafter's buttons from Cranston Collection
- Snow white pearlized dimensional paint from Tulip
- Metallic gold thread
- Liquid Laminate from Beacon
- Batting
- Fusible webbing
- Tacky craft glue
- Air-soluble fabric marker

Decorative Lid Inserts

1. From fabric with Christmas motifs, select a design that will fit in the frame opening. Iron fusible webbing to back of selected design; trim away excess fabric.

2. Using papier-mâché box lid insert as a pattern, cut a piece of the checked fabric. Peel paper backing from fabric design; iron to center of checked fabric, checking to be sure the design will be centered in picture-frame box lid.

3. Apply thin layer of glue to one side of papier-mâché insert; press on fabric with ironed-on design, smoothing carefully to press out any bubbles. Let dry.

4. Highlight design as desired with white pearlized paint; let dry thoroughly.

5. For glossy finish, apply two coats of liquid laminate to fabric, drying thoroughly between coats. Set aside.

Covering Frame Tops

1. Cut an oval ring of scrap fabric same size as top of lid (see Fig. 1). Using fabric cutout as a pattern, cut batting the same size; cut a piece of burgundy fabric with ½" added all around to both inner and outer edges.

2. Layer three pieces—scrap fabric right side down, batting and burgundy fabric right side up. Baste all three lay-

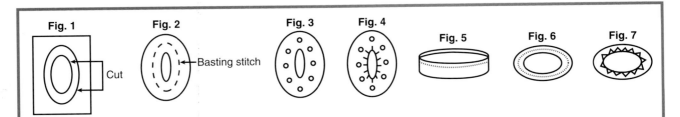

Fig. 1 — Cut

Fig. 2 — Basting stitch

Fig. 3

Fig. 4

Fig. 5

Fig. 6

Fig. 7

ers together with needle and contrasting thread (Fig. 2).

3. Using basting stitches as guide, sew buttons to burgundy fabric using metallic gold thread (Fig. 3). Remove basting stitches.

4. Cut slits in top layer ¼" from inner edge of batting (Fig. 4).

5. Apply bead of glue to upper edge of lid sides (Fig. 5). Smooth glue. Position layered fabric over top of box, smoothing outer edge of fabric over edge of box. Trim away any excess.

6. Apply bead of glue to inside of top of lid (Fig. 6). Draw slitted fabric to inside of lid top (Fig. 7).

7. Apply generous amount of glue to inside of top of lid. Position insert in lid, applying pressure until the insert is set. Let dry.

Finishing Lids

1. Cut batting ½" smaller all around than outer edges of lid. Cut burgundy fabric ½" larger all around than outer edges of lid. Apply bead of glue to inside of lid sides. Layer batting, then fabric over glue, pressing excess fabric evenly around sides of lid.

2. Measure circumference of inside of lid. Cut burgundy fabric strip ½" longer, and ½" wider than lid sides. Press under ¼" hem along one end and one long edge.

3. Apply bead of glue to lower edge of the inside band of lid, being careful not to get glue on flat surface of top. Place strip in lid with hemmed edge inside and to the top, smoothing along entire inside band of lid.

4. Apply a bead of glue to lower outer edge of lid sides. Smooth out glue and fold over raw edge of fabric from inside lid to outside, smoothing it neatly.

5. Measure circumference of outside of lid sides. Cut a strip of burgundy fabric 1" longer, and 1" wider than lid sides. Press under ½" hems along both long edges, and at one end.

6. Apply beads of glue along top and bottom edges of outside of lid sides. Beginning with raw end, apply fabric strip along edge of box lid, overlapping raw edges of fabric folded over edge from inside.

7. Apply a bead of glue around center of lid sides; apply burgundy-and-gold trim. Lid is complete.

Covering Boxes

1. Using bottom of box as pattern, cut checked fabric ½" larger all around. Apply glue around edge of box bottom; smooth out glue and glue fabric to bottom of box, folding edges over onto box sides and smoothing fabric to eliminate wrinkles or bubbles.

2. Measure circumference of box around outside, and height of box side; cut a strip of checked fabric 1" longer and 1" wider. Press under ½" hem along one long edge and at one short end.

3. Apply a bead of glue along lower edge of box side; smooth out glue. Beginning with raw end, apply fabric strip over glue so hem is even with bottom of box. Apply bead of glue along underside of hemmed end; press to box to adhere smoothly and securely.

4. Apply a bead of glue along upper edge inside box; smooth out and neatly fold and press excess fabric over edge to inside of box.

5. Cut a piece of batting ½" smaller all around than inside bottom of box. Cut burgundy fabric ½" larger all around than inside of box bottom. Apply bead of glue to inside of papier-mâché box. Layer batting, then fabric over glue, pressing excess fabric evenly up sides of box.

6. Measure circumference of inside of box; measure height of box side. Cut burgundy fabric strip ½" longer and ½" wider. Press under ¼" hem along both long edges and one end.

7. Apply bead of glue to top and bottom edges of inside of box sides, being carefully to keep glue off covered box bottom. Smooth out glue. Beginning with raw end of burgundy fabric strip, apply fabric strip to inside of box; one hem should be even with top of box and the other should rest smoothly in crease where sides meet bottom of box. Apply glue across hemmed end of strip; press into place. ❈

—Designs by Deborah Spencer Brooks

"I Believe" Santa Wall Hanging

Comfy, cozy felt in country colors works up quickly into an attractive decoration for your home.

Materials
- Kunin Felt:
  9" x 12" denim blue
  9" x 12" navy blue
  9" x 5" cranberry
  Scraps of peach, black and antique gold
- Antique white Plush Felt from Kunin Felt
- 6-strand embroidery floss: black, peach, off-white and navy blue
- ⅝" gold jingle bell
- 6mm black round half-bead
- 5" ½"-diameter imitation evergreen twig
- 10" ¼"-wide red satin ribbon
- 15" curved tree branch
- 2 (⅝") navy blue buttons
- Small amount polyester fiberfill
- Tacky craft glue
- Low-temperature glue gun

Instructions

1. Trim denim blue felt to 7" x 11". From trimmings, cut two hanging loops, 1" x 4½".

2. Referring to patterns (page 163), cut felt as directed. Using pattern and photo as guide, arrange all Santa pieces on denim blue background, overlapping as indicated by dotted lines. Pin in place or "tack" with tiny dabs of craft glue.

3. Using 2 strands peach floss, work Blanket Stitch around portion of hand adjacent to suit and portion of face adjacent to denim blue background. Using 2 strands black, work Blanket Stitch around boots, suit, sleeve and edges of hat adjacent to denim blue background. Using 2 strands off-white, work Blanket Stitch around beard, mustache, hair and trim.

4. Using 4 strands off-white floss and referring to photo throughout, stitch "I Believe" above Santa using a Running Stitch; dot "i" with French Knot.

5. Pin two stars together, matching points. Using 2 strands black floss, join with a running stitch sewn about ⅛" from edges; before closing completely, stuff with a small amount of fiberfill. Complete stitching; repeat with remaining stars.

6. Sew jingle bell to tip of hat. Attach half-round bead to face for eye with craft glue.

7. Bend imitation evergreen into a wreath. Using low-temperature glue gun, carefully glue wreath to wall hanging so it looks like Santa is holding wreath. Tie ribbon in bow; trim ends at an angle and glue bow to wreath.

8. Trim navy blue felt to 7¾" x 11¾". Center completed Santa picture over navy blue felt; pin in place. Using 2 strands navy blue floss, Blanket Stitch picture to navy blue backing.

9. Place one hanging loop over branch; secure to front and back of wall hanging by sewing one of the buttons to front. Repeat for second loop.

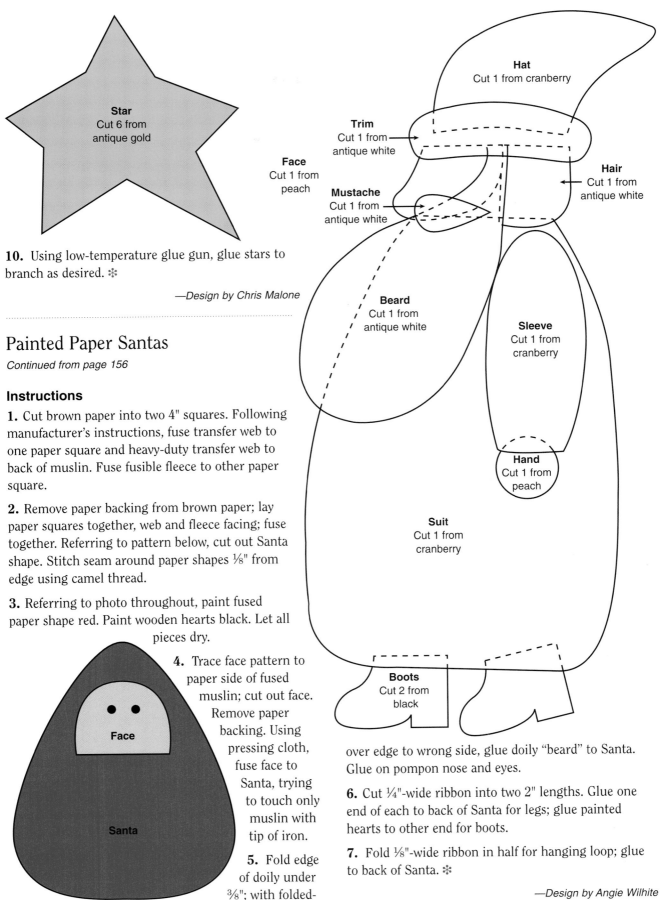

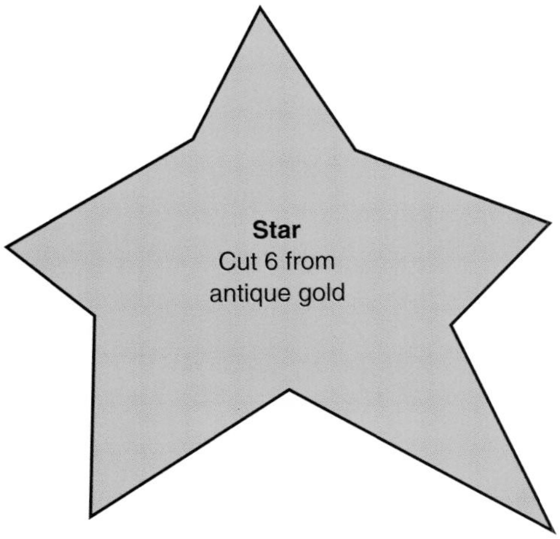
Star
Cut 6 from
antique gold

10. Using low-temperature glue gun, glue stars to branch as desired. ❄

—Design by Chris Malone

Painted Paper Santas

Continued from page 156

Instructions

1. Cut brown paper into two 4" squares. Following manufacturer's instructions, fuse transfer web to one paper square and heavy-duty transfer web to back of muslin. Fuse fusible fleece to other paper square.

2. Remove paper backing from brown paper; lay paper squares together, web and fleece facing; fuse together. Referring to pattern below, cut out Santa shape. Stitch seam around paper shapes ⅛" from edge using camel thread.

3. Referring to photo throughout, paint fused paper shape red. Paint wooden hearts black. Let all pieces dry.

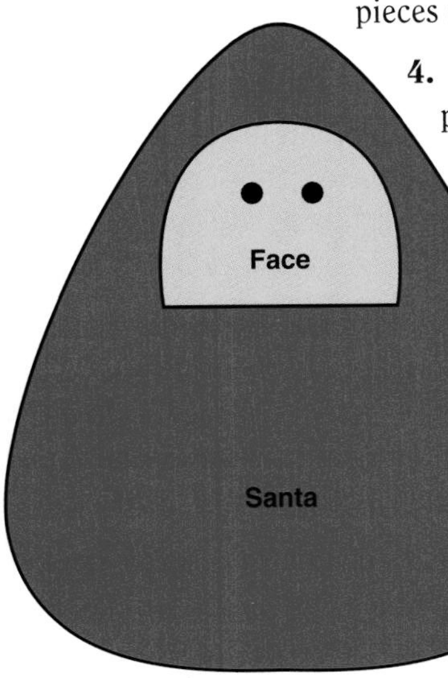
Face
Santa

4. Trace face pattern to paper side of fused muslin; cut out face. Remove paper backing. Using pressing cloth, fuse face to Santa, trying to touch only muslin with tip of iron.

5. Fold edge of doily under ⅜"; with folded-over edge to wrong side, glue doily "beard" to Santa. Glue on pompon nose and eyes.

6. Cut ¼"-wide ribbon into two 2" lengths. Glue one end of each to back of Santa for legs; glue painted hearts to other end for boots.

7. Fold ⅛"-wide ribbon in half for hanging loop; glue to back of Santa. ❄

—Design by Angie Wilhite

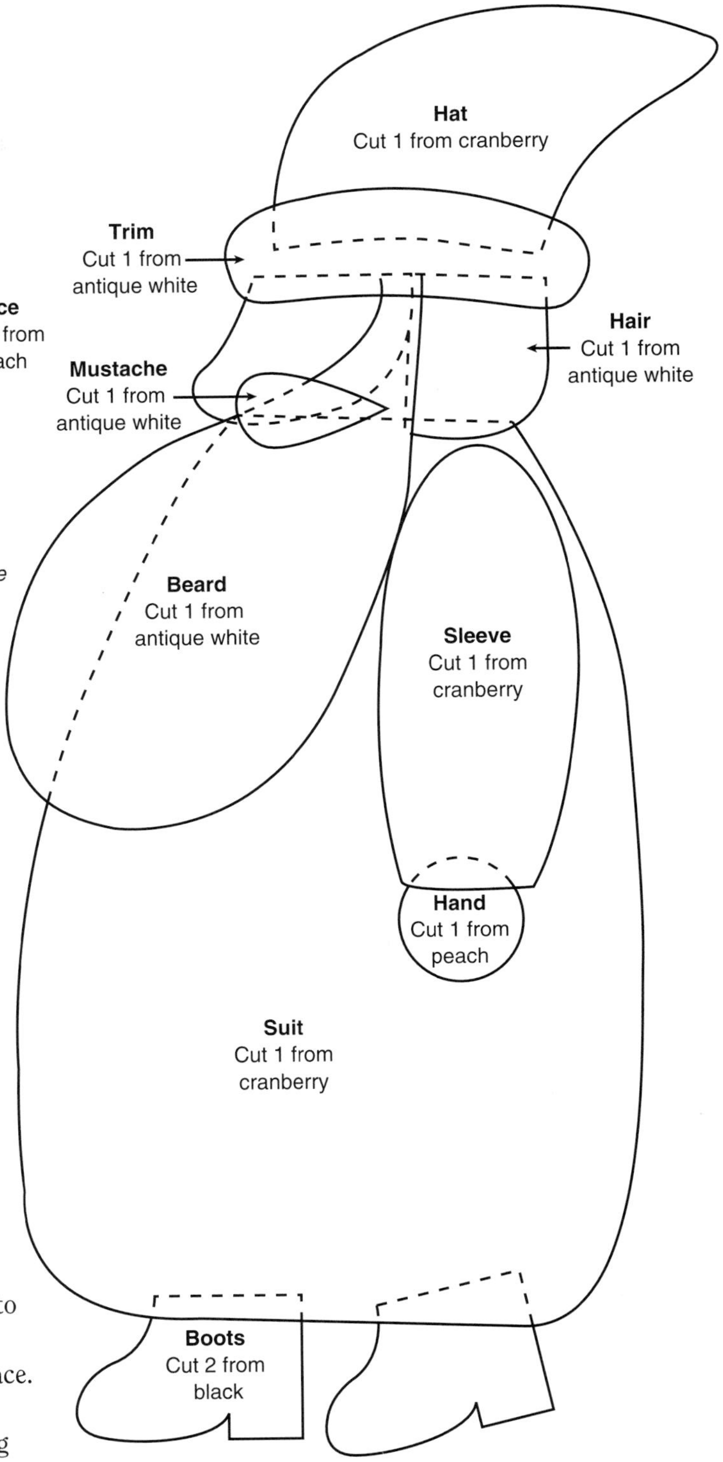
Hat
Cut 1 from cranberry
Trim
Cut 1 from
antique white
Face
Cut 1 from
peach
Mustache
Cut 1 from
antique white
Hair
Cut 1 from
antique white
Beard
Cut 1 from
antique white
Sleeve
Cut 1 from
cranberry
Hand
Cut 1 from
peach
Suit
Cut 1 from
cranberry
Boots
Cut 2 from
black

Holiday Sweatshirt

Multicolored lights and and gingerbread cookies adorn this cuddly sweatshirt.
It's just the thing to wear to your tree-trimming party!

Materials

- Adult white sweatshirt
- Fabric medium
- DecoArt Americana acrylic paints:
  Alizarin crimson
  Bright green
  Burnt umber
  Cadmium orange
  Cadmium yellow
  Holly green
  Lamp (ebony) black
  Lavender
  Raw sienna
  Royal fuchsia

  Royal purple
  Santa red
  Shimmering silver
  Spice pink
  True blue
  Ultra blue
  Viridian green
- Liquitex Concentrated Artists Color paints:
  Opal gold
  Opal green
- Dimensional fabric paints:
  Glossy white
  Glitter white
  Metallic gold

- Paintbrushes from Royal Brush Mfg., Inc.:
  #8 and #12 flat #RG 700
  #3/8 angular #RG 160
  #0 #RG 585
  #1 #RG 250
- Gem-Tac jewel glue from Beacon Chemical
- Red flat-back jewels and assorted other colors
- Heat-sensitive pencil

Project Notes

Mix fabric medium with acrylic paints before applying them to the shirt. This doubles the volume of paint and allows the colors to penetrate the fabric fibers.

Apply an even coat of medium to an area of the design before applying paints to the fabric. This will allow the paint to flow evenly over the design as you are painting.

Add colors for shading and highlighting while the base coats are still wet.

Preparing Sweatshirt & Patterns

1. Launder shirt to remove sizing; do not use fabric softener or dryer sheets.

2. Referring to patterns (page 166), trace gingerbread man, holly leaves and ornament onto tracing paper using regular pencil. Flip patterns over; retrace using heat-sensitive pencil. Place patterns randomly around shirt, right side up, referring to photo as desired, and transfer into place using iron.

Painting

1. Base-coat gingerbread men using raw sienna. Visually divide gingerbread man in half, from middle of head down. Shade one side with burnt umber; highlight the other side with opal gold.

2. Thin spice pink with fabric medium; apply to cheeks using #12 flat brush. Shade a nose between cheeks with burnt umber using angular brush.

3. Using black, paint ovals above each cheek, adding eyelashes and a wavy line for the mouth using liner brush. Add glossy white dot to each eye. (Use alternate eye design as desired.)

4. Using glossy white, add wavy line around edges of gingerbread man. Using handle of paintbrush, place two dots of Santa red paint side by side on gingerbread man; form heart by drawing tip out from drops of paint.

5. Base-coat holly leaves with bright green. Shade leaves that appear underneath and the bottom section of those on top with viridian green; highlight with opal green. Add veins to each leaf using liner brush and viridian green.

6. Base-coat ornaments using Santa red; shade one side with alizarin crimson and highlight other side with glitter white. Paint ornament cap on top of ornament with metallic gold, adding three small dots at base of cap, one at each end and one in middle. Add hanging ring to top of cap.

7. Using pencil, freehand a string for the lights randomly among the gingerbread men, holly leaves and orna-

Continued on page 166

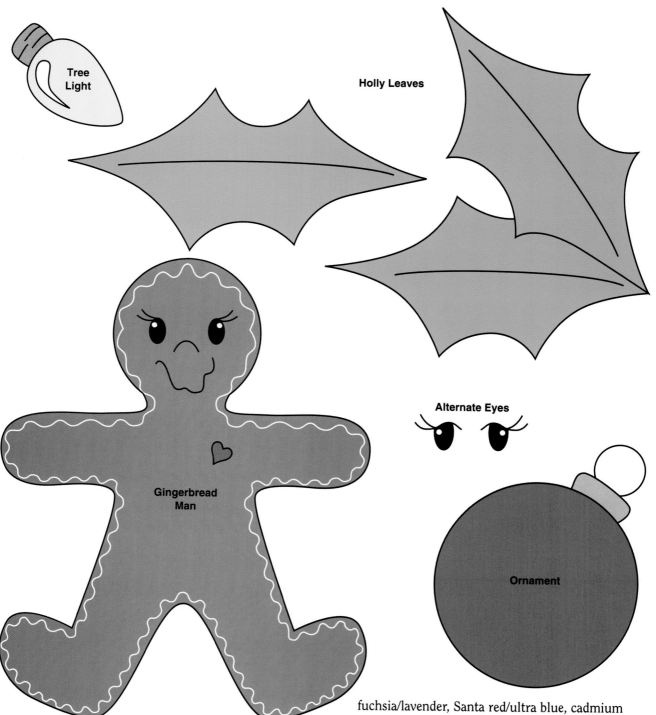

Tree Light

Holly Leaves

Gingerbread Man

Alternate Eyes

Ornament

fuchsia/lavender, Santa red/ultra blue, cadmium orange/Santa red, ultra blue/royal purple and holly green/viridian green.

ments. Transfer tracings of tree lights on both sides of string. Thin black paint with fabric medium and paint string using liner brush. Paint end of each light bulb with shimmering silver, adding three short black lines using a liner brush.

8. Paint light bulbs, base-coating with the first color in each of the following pairs and shading with the second: cadmium yellow/cadmium orange, bright green/viridian green, lavender/royal purple, ultra blue/true blue, royal

9. Using glitter white, add a comma-stroke highlight to each light bulb. Allow paints to dry completely.

10. Referring to photo, glue red gemstones in place for holly berries and highlights on ornaments, and multicolored rhinestones to gingerbread men for buttons as desired. ❋

—Design by Shelia Sommers

Pinecone Tree

Berries and pods add seasonal touches of red and green to this Christmas tree, which is fashioned from small pinecones and frosted with gold.

Materials

- 10" plastic foam cone
- Botanicals from Creative Chi:

  300 hemlock cones

  45 jackie berries

  30 green curly pods

  2 star anise
- Red felt
- True gold #DG37 Ultra Gloss Metallic acrylic paint from DecoArt
- #6 shader "cosmetic" artist's paintbrush #4300 from Loew-Cornell
- Low-temperature glue gun

Instructions

1. Coat plastic foam cone lightly with gold paint; let dry. Paint two star anise; let dry, then glue together back to back.

2. Cut felt to fit base of cone, but do not glue at this time.

3. Beginning at top, glue hemlock cones to plastic foam cone, covering entire tree. Lightly brush tree with gold paint; let dry. Repeat with second light coat of gold paint if desired; let dry.

4. Glue felt to base of tree. Glue green curly pods and jackie berries randomly but evenly over surface of tree. Glue star anise to top of tree. ✻

—Design by Creative Chi

Santa Tangle of Lights

Santa may have a little trouble stringing the lights on his tree, but he's a natural when it comes to brightening your surroundings for Christmas!

Materials

- 7" x 9" x ¾" wood
- Woodsies ¹⁵⁄₁₆" x ³⁄₈" wooden ovals from Forster Inc.
- Ceramcoat acrylic paints from Delta Technical Coatings, Inc.: black, bright red, burnt umber, Christmas green, crocus yellow, fleshtone, 14K gold, gypsy rose, mocha brown, phthalo blue, pumpkin orange and white
- Decorative Snow from Delta Technical Coatings, Inc.
- Sparkle Glaze from Delta Technical Coatings, Inc.
- Acrylic Sealer Gloss from Plaid Enterprises, Inc.
- Paintbrushes
- Fine-tip black permanent marking pen
- 2¼ yards 26-gauge wire
- Scroll saw or band saw
- Drill
- Sandpaper

Instructions

1. Referring to photo and patterns (page 169 and 170) throughout, cut shape from wood using scroll saw or band saw. Sand all edges and surfaces until smooth.

2. Base-coat wood with white paint on both sides and all edges; let dry overnight.

3. Using photo as a guide throughout, paint wooden shape, front, back and on edges. Let painted portions dry before painting adjacent sections.

4. Shade red portions of Santa with mixture of half-drop black and five drops red.

5. Shade beard and mustache with mixture of three drops crocus yellow and one drop water; let dry. Add additional shading to beard and mustache with mixture of half-drop black and five drops white; use same mixture to outline and highlight Santa's boots.

6. Shade Santa's head with mixture of two drops mocha brown and half-drop fleshtone.

7. Shade mittens and tree with mixture of three drops green and half-drop black.

8. Let painted piece dry overnight after all shading has been added. Referring to pattern, add final details and highlights with black fine-tip pen. Apply decorative snow liberally to "fur" on Santa's suit; let dry overnight.

Finishing & Assembly

1. Drill holes through wood where indicated (circles on pattern), drilling only halfway into wood at "electrical outlet" beside Santa's boot (star on pattern).

Lights

Front

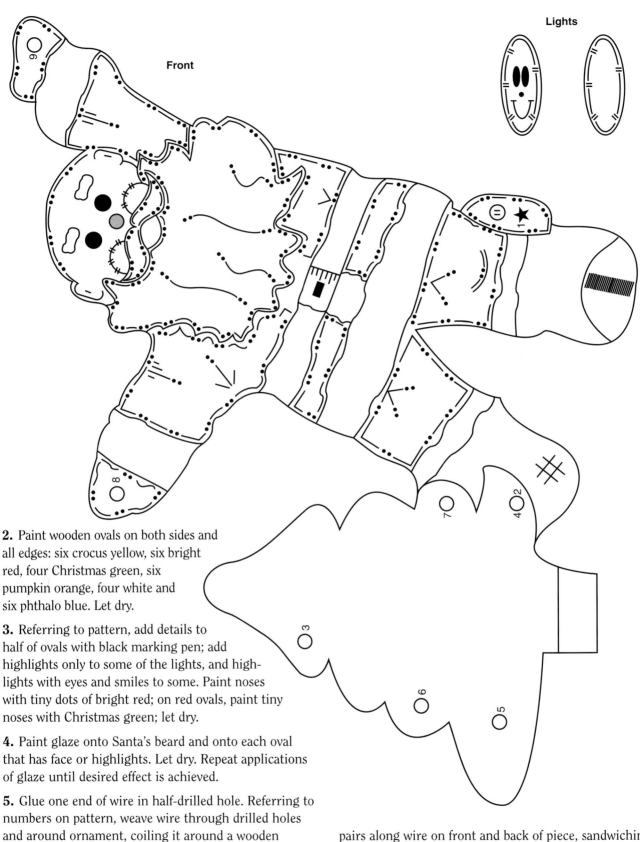

2. Paint wooden ovals on both sides and all edges: six crocus yellow, six bright red, four Christmas green, six pumpkin orange, four white and six phthalo blue. Let dry.

3. Referring to pattern, add details to half of ovals with black marking pen; add highlights only to some of the lights, and highlights with eyes and smiles to some. Paint noses with tiny dots of bright red; on red ovals, paint tiny noses with Christmas green; let dry.

4. Paint glaze onto Santa's beard and onto each oval that has face or highlights. Let dry. Repeat applications of glaze until desired effect is achieved.

5. Glue one end of wire in half-drilled hole. Referring to numbers on pattern, weave wire through drilled holes and around ornament, coiling it around a wooden paintbrush handle as you go. Add wire hanging loop through holes in Santa's mittens.

6. Glue highlighted and plain painted lights together in

pairs along wire on front and back of piece, sandwiching wire between ovals.

7. Spray piece with acrylic sealer gloss; let dry. ✳

—*Design by Chris Brack*

Back

Joyful Bear

Continued from page 157

2. Flatten one end of each leg to attach to body. Shape foot at other end by pinching bottom of leg and then rounding it.

3. Attach legs to indentation at bottom of body; make heels touch.

Wreath, Wings & Joy

1. Roll a pea-size ball of green compound into a 1½"-long rope. Flatten rope slightly and twist it. Starting at back of head, wrap wreath over top of bear's head and around one ear; trim excess where ends meet in back.

2. Roll six tiny balls of red compound for berries; attach to wreath in two clusters of three berries.

3. Roll two marble-size balls of ivory compound for wings; flatten and shape each into a teardrop. Shape the tip so it curves upward slightly. Compare wings; each should be about 1¼" long.

Kissing Ball

A delicate crocheted doily gives this vintage holiday decoration plenty of Victorian charm. Hang it up, then step beneath it and kiss your sweetie for luck!

Materials

- Annie's Collection 12" round white crocheted doily #PR002W12 from Peking Handicraft
- Several silk or paper red roses with leaves
- 2-part 100mm clear plastic ball with hanging loop
- Sprigs of red berries
- Gold spray paint
- Gold acrylic paint
- White sewing thread
- Thin gold cord
- Low-temperature glue gun

Instructions

1. Spray plastic ball inside and out with gold spray paint. Brush gold acrylic paint lightly on edges of rose leaves and petals. Let ball and roses dry.

2. Slip gold cord through hanging loop; knot.

3. Using needle and thread, run gathering thread around periphery of doily. Pull to gather doily around ball. Knot thread through hanging loop; secure with a dot of glue.

4. Glue berries, leaves and roses to top of ball. ❈

—Design by Beth Wheeler

4. Press wings together firmly at rounded end; center on bear's back and press on firmly. Incise three lines on each wing with straight edge.

5. Shape marble-size ball of yellow compound into a 4"-long rope. Flatten rope slightly and twist.

6. From rope, cut three 1"-long pieces. Form one piece into the J, one into an O, and the third into the longest piece of the Y; cut a separate ½"-long section from rope to make the shorter part of the Y. Press letters together; place in bear's paws against stomach.

Finishing

1. Curve wire over a paintbrush handle; cut ends and push U-shaped wire into top of bear's head for hanger.

2. Transfer molded figure to an oven-proof plate. Bake in a preheated 275-degree oven for 10 minutes; cool completely.

3. Place figure on cardboard; spray front of bear with spray glitter. Let dry completely before handling. ❈

—Design by Jackie Haskell

Christmas Wreath

You can make this colorful holiday wreath quickly, and enjoy it year after year!

Materials

- Aleene's Premium-Coat Acrylics acrylic paints:
  True red #OC 103
  Dusty green #OC 141
  Dusty blue #OC 153
  Dusty violet #OC 165
- Aleene's Essentials paints:
  Ivory #OC 179

  Yellow ochre #OC 184
- Aleene's Enhancers paint products:
  Satin varnish #EN 102
  All-purpose primer #EN 104
- Paintbrushes:
  ¼" flat brush
  ¾" flat brush
  #0 liner brush

  #1 round brush
- Sponge stencil brush
- Stylus (optional)
- Mini-tweed stencil #41-5060 from Provo Craft
- Fine-grain sandpaper
- Thick tacky craft glue
- 18" grapevine or twig wreath
- 15 (½") 2-hole buttons

- Wooden cutouts:
  3 (6" x 2") primitive-style Christmas trees
  3 (1⅜"-wide) primitive-style stars
  2 (1") stars
  2" primitive-style star

1" x 1⅞" primitive-style heart
¾" x 1" primitive-style heart
⅛"-thick 2½" square
2 (⅛"-thick) 2" squares
¼"-thick 3" x 5" rectangle
¼"-thick 3" x 1¼" rectangle

- 2 (1½") wooden cubes
- Craft drill
- Craft wire
- Jute twine
- Natural raffia

Project Notes

Refer to photo throughout for color placement.

Thinned paints are used to decorate some painted wooden pieces. To thin paint, mix color indicated with water to a milky consistency.

Painting

1. Mix one part primer with one part water; apply mixture to all wooden shapes. Let dry; sand lightly.

2. Using ¾" flat brush, base-coat as follows: trees and two buttons, dusty green; stars, one button and 2½" square, yellow ochre; one cube and smaller rectangle, dusty blue; one cube and one 2" square, dusty violet; and one 2" square, both hearts and larger rectangle, true red. Set pieces aside to dry as needed so that all sides and edges can be painted.

3. *Trees:* Mix three parts dusty green with one part ivory. Position stencil over painted tree. Dip sponge into paint; pounce on palette to blend, and press through stencil. Repeat on other trees, using different pattern for each.

4. *Yellow ochre square:* Using #1 round brush, paint undiluted dusty green trees on yellow ochre square.

5. *Dusty blue cube:* Using ¼" flat brush and thinned ivory, pull vertical lines on cube; let dry. Using #0 liner brush and thinned dusty violet, pull vertical and horizontal lines on cube to resemble plaid design.

6. *Dusty blue rectangle:* Using ¼" flat brush and thinned true red, paint three stripes across rectangle. Using #0 liner brush and thinned yellow ochre, paint two stripes next to each red stripe.

7. *Dusty violet square:* Dot undiluted yellow ochre and true red onto surface with stylus or tip of wooden paintbrush handle.

8. *Red rectangle:* Using #0 liner brush and undiluted ivory, paint lettering. Using #1 round brush and thinned ochre, paint stars and highlight lettering.

9. *Red square:* Using #0 liner brush and thinned yellow ochre, paint small spirals over surface of square.

10. *Dusty violet cube:* Using #1 round brush and thinned yellow ochre, paint stars over surface of cube.

11. Using ¾" brush, coat all painted pieces with satin varnish.

Finishing & Assembly

1. Drill two holes (as for a button) through centers of stars, at top centers of hearts and trees, and in center of dusty blue rectangle.

2. Lay larger heart atop largest star; thread wire from back through both pieces; twist on front to hold pieces together. Coil wire ends around paintbrush handle; weave ends through holes in green buttons.

3. Lay one of smallest stars atop dusty blue rectangle. Thread wire from back through both pieces; twist on front. Coil wire ends around paintbrush handle.

4. Lay medium star atop each tree. Thread wire from back through both pieces; twist on front. Coil wire ends around paintbrush handle.

5. Weave one piece wire each through yellow ochre button, remaining smallest star and smaller heart; twist wire ends across front and coil ends around paintbrush handle.

6. Using jute twine, wrap "ribbons" around cubes and squares, tying ends in bows. Glue wired heart atop bow on dusty purple square, and wired yellow ochre button atop bow on red square. Tie jute bow and glue to upper left corner of red rectangle; glue remaining wired star atop bow.

7. Make wire-on anchors for painted pieces by threading 8"–12" piece of wire through remaining buttons so wire ends extend out back (rounded side) of buttons. Glue front (flat side) of buttons to backs of wooden pieces, using two on each tree and red rectangle, and one on other pieces. Let dry completely.

8. Tie large raffia bow at 2 o'clock position on wreath. Wire wooden shapes to wreath. Add wire hanging loop to back of wreath. ✳

—Design by Judy Malone

Pinecone Wreath

Dried natural materials make a beautiful holiday wreath. Armed with a low-temperature glue gun, you can complete this holiday classic in next to no time!

Materials

- 6" bago bago wreath
- Natural raffia
- Paddle wire
- Botanicals from Creative Chi:
  4 senna pods
  2 bunches pepper berries
- Casurina pods tipped with white paint: 2 large, 2 small
- 2 eucalyptus leaves
- 2 sprigs white German statice
- 3 star anise
- Birch cones: 2 large, 2 small
- 10 rose hips
- 2 thin 4" twigs
- 4 (3"-long) cinnamon sticks
- Low-temperature glue gun

Instructions

1. Hold several strands of raffia together; tie in 3½"-wide bow. Wire bow to center of left side of wreath, concealing wire in raffia.

2. Working outward from bow and referring to photo throughout, glue on senna pods, pepper berries, large casurina pods, twigs, cinnamon sticks and eucalyptus leaves. Add the small casurina pods, German statice, star anise and large birch cones. Fill in with small birch cones and rose hips.

3. Add wire hanging loop to top center on back of wreath. ✳

—*Design by Creative Chi*

Shopper's Guide

Special thanks to the following manufacturers who provided the designers with product for their projects. To find materials listed, first check your local craft and retail stores. If you are unable to locate a product locally, contact the manufacturers below for the closest retail source in your area.

A Bear in Sheep's Clothing
P.O. Box 770
Medford, MA 02155

Adhesive Technologies, Inc.
3 Merrill Industrial Dr.
Hampton, NH 03842-1995
(603) 926-1616

Aleene's
85 Industrial Way
Buellton, CA 93427
(800) 436-7878

BagWorks, Inc.
3933 California Pky. E.
Fort Worth, TX 76119-7340
(817) 536-3892

Beacon Chemical/ Signature Mktg. & Mfg.
230 Everett Ave.
Wyckoff, NJ 07481
(201) 848-1818

Binney & Smith, Inc./Liquitex
1100 Church Ln.
Easton, PA 18044
(610) 253-6271

Charles Craft, Inc.
P.O. Box 1049
Laurinburg, NC 28353
(919) 844-3521

Coats & Clark
30 Patewood Dr., Suite 351
Greenville, SC 29615
(803) 234-0331

Creative Beginnings
475 Morro Bay Blvd.
Morro Bay, CA 93442
(805) 772-9030

Creative Chi
8608 Kratz Ln.
Baltimore, MD 21244
(410) 922-9110

Daniel Enterprises
P.O. Box 1105
Laurinburg, NC 28353
(910) 277-7441

Darice, Inc.
21160 Drake Rd.
Strongsville, OH 44136
(216) 238-9150

DecoArt
P.O. Box 360
Stanford, KY 40484
(800) 367–3047

Delta Technical Coatings,
2550 Pellissier Pl.
Whittier, CA 90601-1505
(800) 423-4135

DMC Corp.
10 Port Kearny
South Kearny, NJ 07032-4688
(201) 589-0606

Duncan Enterprises
5673 E. Shields Ave.
Fresno, CA 93727
(209) 291-4444

Fiber Mosaics
509 S. Kellogg
Kennewick, WA 99336
(509) 735-1463

Forster Inc.
P.O. Box 657
Wilton, ME 04294-0657
(207) 645-2574

Jesse James & Co.
615 N. New St.
Allentown, PA 18102

JHB International, Inc.
1955 S. Quince St.
Denver, CO 80231
(303) 751–8100

Kreinik Mfg. Co., Inc.
3601 Timanus Ln., Suite 101
Baltimore, MD 21244
(800) 537-2166

Krylon/Illinois Bronze
31500 Solon Rd.
Solon, OH 44139-3908
(216) 498-3283

Kunin Felt
380 Lafayette Rd.
Hampton, NH 03842-5000
(800) 292-7900

Lara's Crafts (Div. of Woodworks)
4220 Clay Ave.
Fort Worth, TX 76117
(817) 581-9493

Lion Ribbon Co.
Rte. 24, Box 601
Chester, NJ 07930-0601
(908) 879-4700

Loew-Cornell, Inc.
563 Chestnut Ave.
Teaneck, NJ 07666
(201) 729-6323

Madeira Marketing, Inc.
600 E. Ninth
Michigan City, IN 46360
(219) 8731000

Mill Hill Gay Bowles Sales, Inc.
1310 Plainfield Ave.
Janesville, WI 53545
(608) 754-9466

C.M. Offray & Son
Rte. 24
Chester, NJ 07930-0601
(908) 879-4700

One & Only Creations (Avtor)
P.O. Box 2730
Napa, CA 94558
(707) 255-8033

Peking Handicraft
1388 San Mateo
South San Francisco, CA 94080
(415) 871-3788

Pellon Div./Freudenberg Nonwovens
20 Industrial Ave.
Chelmsford, MA 01824
(508) 454-0461

Plaid Enterprises, Inc.
1649 International Ct.
Norcross, GA 30091-7600
(404) 923-8200

Provo Craft
285 E 900 S
Provo, UT 84606
(801) 377-4311

Rainbow Gallery mail order:
Designs by Joan Green
6345 Fairfield Rd.
Oxford, OH 45056
(513) 523-2690

Robert Simmons, Inc.
45 W. 18th St.
New York, NY 10011
(212) 675-3136

Royal Brush Mfg., Inc.
6949 Kennedy Ave.
Hammond, IN 46323
(219) 845-5666

Therm O Web
770 Glenn Ave.
Wheeling, IL 60090
(708) 520-5200

Tulip, Div. of Polymerics
24 Prime Park Way
Natick, MA 01760
(508) 650-5400

Uniek, Inc.
805 Uniek Dr.
Waunakee, WI 53597
(608) 849-9999

V.I.P. Fabrics
1412 Broadway
New York, NY 10018
(800) 847-4064

Westwater Enterprises
917 Mountain Ave.
Mountainside, NJ 07092
(908) 654-8871

Wimpole Street Creations
419 W 500 S
Bountiful, UT 84010
(801) 298-0504

Wright's
85 South St.
West Warren, MA 01092
(800) 628-9362

Project Index

Designer Index